Eating The Chocolate Elephant

Take Charge of Change
Through Total Process Management℠

By Mark D. Youngblood

Written by Mark D. Youngblood.

Cover art by Creative Support.

Page design and illustrations by Kyrsten Johnson, Perfect Page.

Produced by Perfect Page.

Quotations not attributed to anyone are by the author. Quotations by others are noted in the "Notes" section at the end or are taken from *Bartlett's Book of Business Quotations*.

Micrografx, Inc.
1303 Arapaho
Richardson, Texas 75081
Sales and Marketing: (214) 234-1769   Part Number RM3140

CONTENTS

INTRODUCTION

TPM FOUNDATION

TPM Part 1: Establish Commitment to Total Process Management

TPM Part 2: Create Process Improvement Capability

TPM PROCESS IMPROVEMENT CYCLE

TPM Part 3: Evaluate the Current Environment

TPM Part 4: Conduct Benchmarking

TPM Part 5: Establish Customer-Driven Stretch Goals

TPM Part 6: Brainstorm Innovations

TPM Part 7: Implement Innovations

CONCLUSION

LIST OF FIGURES

Chapter 1

Chapter 2

Chapter 3

Chapter 4

Chapter 5

Chapter 6

Chapter 7

Chapter 8

Chapter 9

Chapter 10

Chapter 11

Chapter 12

Chapter 13

Chapter 14

Chapter 15

Chapter 16

No numbered figures

Chapter 17

Chapter 18

Chapter 19

Chapter 20

No numbered figures

PREFACE

In recent years, the pace of change has increased exponentially, and competitive pressures from around the world have appeared virtually overnight. Unfortunately, very few companies have navigated successfully through these changes. The primary purpose of this book is to help companies manage change successfully. Management experts have always touted approaches for improving corporate performance (called *change management*), which have proven effective to greater or lesser extents. Despite having the benefit of proven change management approaches, companies continually fail in their efforts to improve corporate performance. Why should that be the case? From my experience, I have seen that the primary reason for failure has been *lack of effective execution*. In this book, I hope to solve some of these problems by providing a detailed method for managing organizational change.

Over a decade ago, the quality movement established a beachhead in corporate America, and has grown steadily ever since. Now, quality's supremacy is being challenged by an upstart called Business Process Reengineering. Despite the fact that both are excellent approaches for managing change, most companies are doing one *or* the other. In those few companies that are doing both, a war is being waged between the two factions over who has the best approach. The second purpose of this book is to stop that war. Total Process Management℠ (TPM) provides a single methodology that integrates the best of both Total Quality Management and Business Process Reengineering and gives companies a *complete* approach to managing organizational change.

The seven-part Total Process Management methodology grew out of nearly two decades of direct experience in implementing organizational change. Having worked in a number of corporate environments and in professional consulting, I have personally lived through the struggle to articulate and implement change. I learned that most people can accept even dramatic change if they understand the need to change, believe in the method for change, and feel that they are participating in the change. The Total Process Management methodology reflects these lessons and provides a road map for successful change from the "boardroom to the mailroom."

Please provide your feedback on the Total Process Management methodology to The MetaSys Change Management Group, or call (800) 998-1981.

Mark D. Youngblood
December, 1993
Richardson, Texas USA

Acknowledgments:
Special thanks go to my wife Connie and son Ryan for their love and understanding during the long hours I was away writing this book. Thanks to Kent Odland for his contributions to the material and to Gordon Tucker for making this dream possible. Thanks to Gordon Sellers for sharing the dream. Thanks to Kareen Strickler for her timely wisdom and insight. Last, thanks to all of the volunteers who read early drafts of the book and provided the invaluable feedback that contributed to the quality of this book.

INTRODUCTION

INTRODUCTION 1

"Turn and face the strange changes."
      —David Bowie

Imagine a chocolate elephant. Four thousand pounds of solid chocolate — ten feet high at the shoulder, fifteen feet long, eight feet across — and it is your job to eat it.

The idea of eating a chocolate elephant is so monumentally staggering that it is hard to know where or how to start. This is what it feels like for most people when faced with trying to manage organizational change. Many companies put off starting performance improvement — people just keep telling each other that they "really should eat that chocolate elephant" (someday). Other companies try to eat the chocolate elephant in one bite and nearly destroy the company in the process. Still others will start and stop with change efforts so often that they never make any progress. These companies lack a reliable approach for managing organizational change.

The need for businesses to adopt a change management approach is greater now than ever before. "The era of revolutionary corporate change — still just beginning — promises enormous economic improvements at an excep-

3

tionally high cost in human pain. Make no mistake: Companies *must* transform themselves radically to survive and become more competitive."[1] In recent years the pace of change has accelerated, and there is no end in sight. The problem is not with change itself but with the fact that companies do not manage change effectively. *If you don't control change, it will control you.* It's that simple.

Most companies are ill equipped to handle organizational change. The *Harvard Business Review* reports that, "The problem for most executives is that managing change is unlike any other managerial task they have ever confronted. When it comes to change, the model he uses for organizational issues doesn't work."[2] The results from a recent Gallup poll support this statement. The survey showed that many people believe that their organization is changing rapidly, but more than half of them think that their company cannot handle the change. Only one percent of executives surveyed said that they use a formal change management structure. This suggests that as much as 99% of all companies do not have an organized approach for adapting to our changing times![3]

> *He that will not apply new remedies must expect new evils; for time is the greatest innovator.*
> — *Francis Bacon*

> *"Change is not something that happens. It's a way of life. It's not a process, it's a value. It's not something you do, it engulfs you."*[4]
> — *Ronald E. Compton CEO,*
> *Aetna Life and Casualty*

One of the new business rules for the 21st century is that companies must build permanent change into the fabric of the business. Experts predict that in the future successful companies will be best described as "adaptive." In these companies change will replace stability as a key trait. Successful companies will recognize that what works today will likely not work tomorrow: "There's an awareness that the reinvention of the corporation is going to go on forever."[4] Dr. Michael Hammer adds, " . . . the hallmark of a really successful company is the ability to abandon what has been successful in the past."[5] One of the keys to Motorola's success has been an "evangelical commitment to change that has permeated all levels of the company."[6] To be successful, companies must adopt an approach to support rapid and deliberate change. The CEO of General Electric, John F. Welch, tells the following story:

> *People always ask, "Is the change over? Can we stop now?" You've got to tell them, "No, it's just begun." They must come to understand that it is never ending. Leaders must create an atmosphere where people understand that change is a continuing process, not an event.*[7]

It is no problem finding ideas about how a business should change. The problem is that there are too many. For example, a recent publication describes 25 different management tools and techniques![8] How are business leaders supposed to wade through the dizzying array of change approaches being touted in today's press? The approaches and people shown in Figure 1.1 represent just a part of the offerings available. Is it any wonder that most business managers today are dazed by change?

Most companies do not succeed with change management, whether the approaches are Total Quality Management, Business Process Reengineering or something else. According to one estimate, as many as 70% of Business Process Reengineering efforts fail,[9] and similar results are reported for quality improvement programs.[10] Unfortunately,

5

Figure 1.1

How are business
leaders supposed
to wade through
the dizzying array
of change
approaches being
touted in
today's press?

the business problems that they were targeted to solve will not go away by themselves—something still must be done.

Starting over a decade ago with approaches such as management by objectives (MBO) and quality circles, change management fads have deluged companies until many people today are numb to them. Executives try an approach until it doesn't deliver results quickly enough and then switch to the next approach. Employees take an attitude to "wait and see" if management is serious this time, and that undermines the credibility of the change effort.[11] These "change survivors" are cynical people who have learned how to beat the system by waiting out the change movement without changing at all.[12]

> The Public . . . demands
> certainties . . . But there are *no*
> certainties.
>
> — *H.L. Mencken*

One problem is that most change management approaches are presented as the exclusive path to corporate change. Whether the approach is Business Process Reengineering,

Total Quality Management, organizational development, benchmarking, or the learning organization, businesses are told that only one of these approaches is the right solution. So what happens when the approach isn't broad enough to accommodate all the types of change experienced by companies of different sizes and in different competitive circumstances? Usually, the change approach is viewed as unsuccessful and replaced with another approach in a never-ending cycle. Actually, most change management approaches are not intrinsically ineffective; however, they are either poorly executed or are simply not a total solution.

Process reengineering, benchmarking, Total Quality Management, broad banding, worker empowerment, skill-based pay. The labels abound when it comes to trendy remedies executives are using to breathe new life and competitive fire into their companies. But while these approaches may promise more motivated work forces and greater productivity, the results often fall far short. When this happens, companies must sharply modify, abandon or find antidotes to programs that bring sweeping changes to organizational and human-resource management.[13]

Total Process Management (TPM) integrates the best of each of the leading approaches into a single solution. These approaches are more similar than they are dissimilar and none is complete without the balancing strengths of the other approaches. TPM combines the dramatic improvements of process reengineering with the sustaining action of continuous process improvement. It focuses on all the organizational levers for change, including the people issues traditionally addressed through organizational development. TPM

The wave of the future is coming and there is no fighting it.
— *Anne Morrow Lindbergh*

emphasizes benchmarking as an integral activity, and incorporates learning organization concepts into continuous improvement. This synthesis of the leading theories provides a total approach to managing business processes.

Total Process Management is not an exclusive solution. Although it is a complete approach, it need not replace effective change management approaches currently being used. It will complement most other change management approaches that have a narrower focus, because it addresses change across the entire continuum, from dramatic to incremental.

In implementing change programs, too many companies confuse the means with the end. They make the mistake of "equating the measures of activities with actual improvements in performance. Companies proclaim their quality programs with the same pride with which they would proclaim real performance improvements."[14] The purpose of Total Process Management is to *deliver process improvement results.* TPM is the means, *not* the end.

Companies often sacrifice near-term results for the promise from process improvement approaches of long-term benefits that may never happen. TPM delivers both short-term and long-term improvement *results*. The design of the TPM methodology is to provide immediate, goal-specific results as well as long-term gradual improvements. Today's improvements need not be delayed for some problematic tomorrow. Also, TPM avoids sacrificing the future on the altar of today's benefits. Long-term improvements are built onto short-term successes to ensure continued performance improvement.

The purpose of this book is to provide a framework for action — for *eating the chocolate elephant.* The seven-part Total Process Management methodology is a complete approach for managing change and achieving performance excellence. It emphasizes structured change, communication, employee involvement, and proven process improvement methods. The key advantages of the TPM methodology are summarized below.

❖ TPM addresses the full range of change from continuous, incremental change to dramatic, discontinuous change.

❖ TPM addresses all of the organizational levers for change: process, systems, structure, and people.

❖ TPM can be integrated with existing change management approaches to provide a complete solution without losing momentum or previous investment in training.

❖ TPM is an approach that delivers both short-term, quick wins and long-term, sustained improvement.

❖ TPM originates from the front line of change where the work gets done. It was developed from real-life experiences about what works and what doesn't. TPM is about delivering results.

BIRTH OF THE CHOCOLATE ELEPHANT 2

Sources of Inefficiency and Poor Performance

"The times they are a-changin."
— Bob Dylan

Welcome to the incredible shrinking world! In this age, each day introduces new competitive pressures from every point of the globe. This is a different experience from that of the early post-World War II years. During that time, America had little competition, resources were plentiful, labor was cheap, and as Michael Hammer puts it, "Any moron could make money in that environment."[1] The mechanistic approach to management, the industrial management model, was thriving and the future seemed secure.

 Somewhere in the 1960s, the fairy tale ended. Shift to the 1970s, enter Japan and Germany with shockingly high quality goods at low prices. This new invasion spawned the American quality revolution, which benefited many

companies, but is still struggling for acceptance today. The threat is not diminishing — shift to the 1990s, enter the European Community, China, India, and the emerging Eastern Bloc. The competitive stakes are being raised each day, and the companies that do not keep up with change are destined to fail. This is reinforced by the following words of one CEO:

> *You've got to be on the cutting edge of change. You can't simply maintain the status quo, because somebody's always coming from another country with another product, or consumer tastes change, or the cost structure does, or there's a technology breakthrough. If you're not fast and adaptable, you're vulnerable. This is true for every segment of every business in every country in the world.[2]*

Figure 2.1

What company names would you label these various dinosaurs with?

THE FAR SIDE   By GARY LARSON

Many companies worldwide are ill equipped to compete effectively. These companies are bloated with management and administrative overhead. Their centralized decision-making strangles responsiveness. Quality is poor, customer awareness is weak, and costs are high. CEOs in these companies are asking, "How did we get in this shape, and what can we do about it?"

Most of today's problems started as yesterday's solutions. For example, industrial management theory was one of the greatest business solutions in recent history, but now it is the leading cause of diminishing competitive capability. "Both the theory and practice of Western management have created a drag on our forward motion. It is the principles of management that are in need of reform."[3]

No idea is so antiquated that it was not once modern. No idea is so modern that it will not someday be antiquated.
— Ellen Glasgow

During the birth of the industrial age, business leaders faced difficult circumstances. The general population was uneducated and illiterate. The emerging industrial technologies were complex and required knowledgeable decision making.[4] How were businesses to reconcile these conditions?

The answer was job segmentation and a "command and control" management style. If you have simple workers, create simple jobs. The solution was the creation of individual jobs with work broken into small, easily taught, and repetitive components. These simple jobs required complex processes to ensure that work flowed smoothly and promptly through the many hand-offs between individuals and departments. Educated supervisors with *super vision* managed these complex processes where information passed up the chain of command and decisions passed back down.

Figure 2.2

Command and
control manage-
ment worked
well in the early
1900s, but does
it still work in
the 1990s, the
Information Age?

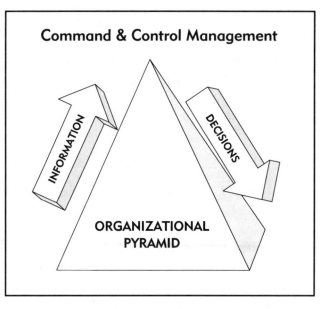

Command & Control Management

INFORMATION

DECISIONS

**ORGANIZATIONAL
PYRAMID**

Guess what? It worked great. However, that was 1900, and this is nearly the 21st century — the Information Age. Does it still work today? NO! Rather than simple jobs and complex processes, we need complex jobs and simple processes. Complex jobs require independent thought and judgment. These jobs are generally more personally fulfilling and require educated workers. Simple processes are efficient, adaptable, and easily understood.

Ad hoc solutions are the second greatest culprit in how our processes became so inefficient. Businesses are full of smart people solving business problems every day. Some of these solutions are so successful that they become institutionalized and people cease to question them. Over time, layers of ad hoc solutions accumulate until you end up with a massive, inefficient, and complex process that has taken on a life of its own — a chocolate elephant.

Over time, ad hoc solutions accumulate into a massive, inefficient, and complex process — a chocolate elephant.

Business management has proven to be quite resourceful in responding to the need for change. Unfortunately, management has been choosing ineffective approaches. Traditionally, businesses respond to the need to change with one of three approaches: reduce headcount, implement new technology, or reorganize.

REDUCE HEADCOUNT

Pick up any paper or business magazine and you will find a story about some company slashing jobs. Usually the first move a new CEO makes in a business turnaround situation is to lay off a large percentage of employees. The reason: "We have to get these labor costs under control" or "We have to get rid of that layer of fat." *Where is this mythical layer of fat?* If by "layers of fat" we mean tasks or activities that do not add value from the customer's perspective, then we are all guilty, from the CEO on down. The problem is that the "fat" (non-value added activities) is epidemic throughout companies — our goal is to remove it wherever it exists.

Slashing jobs without changing the underlying processes does not solve problems, it creates them. Layoffs destroy any trust or good will that a company has built up.[5] One CEO lamented to me that the family atmosphere, a hallmark of his company since its inception, evaporated after a series of layoffs. He said, "The first layoff came as a shock, but the employees were willing to forgive. The second layoff ended any chance of ever going back — we had become a company of hardened, cynical survivors."

All the work is still there, and still must be done. Only now you have fewer employees to do the work. So what happens? Either the work doesn't get done and production suffers, or you end up hiring the labor back. In case after case, the same pattern is repeated. Following large-scale layoffs the original employees are hired back as "contractors" (usually for more money than they were making before) or the positions are recreated within a year. M. Anthony Burns, chairman of Ryder Systems, Inc., summarizes the point, "You just can't summarily lay off people. You've got to change the processes and drive out the unnecessary work, or it will be back tomorrow."[6]

Early retirement programs can be an even worse idea. Although on the surface they look like a humane way to reduce staffing costs, they can be a prescription for dismantling the organization's talent pool. Who do you think can afford to take early retirement offers? Usually the people who are confident they can obtain another job. Who are they? Your best performers, of course! This leaves your already troubled organization without the top performers to lead the way. IBM is one company that learned this lesson. Initially, hiring back early-retirement workers as contractors was thought to be a good idea. Then IBM realized the mixed message that was sent to the remaining employees. If the work was supposed to be eliminated, why were contractors being hired to do the work?[7] Early retirement programs must be structured so that employees with key skills or knowledge are not allowed to leave.

IMPLEMENT NEW TECHNOLOGY

Business Week (June 14, 1993) reports that in the past decade over a trillion dollars have been spent on information technology. Others estimate that the actual number may be many times that. Clearly, we have not seen a corresponding increase in productivity. Why not? To understand this phenomenon, let's review briefly the history of information systems development.

Until the late 1970s most computer systems were developed to process work in batches. The automation requirement resulted in organizing work processes to deliver batched work output. This fit well with compartmentalized operations where portions of the work were done in separate areas and passed from person to person until the work was completed. As computing technology evolved, increasingly more information could be entered and validated on-line, thus providing opportunity for work efficiencies. However, the underlying work habits did not change. People still wrote the information down, batched it up, and then keyed it in on-line.

Where are the corresponding increases in productivity from the trillion dollars businesses have spent on information technology over the last 10 years?

This illustrates the fundamental reason that new systems and technology haven't delivered on the promised efficiencies — they simply automated the same old ways of doing things. In an area just south of Dallas, Texas, the rural roads were built after people had established their property lines. These roads are miserable to drive because you cannot go more than a few hundred yards before you have to make a 90-degree turn to go around someone's property. This is what we do with our system development — we design the systems around established "property lines."

The popular expression for this is "paving the cow path," which means putting a highway where the cows used to walk. These are the conditions that led to Michael Hammer's landmark article in the *Harvard Business Review* (July-

August, 1990) titled "Reengineering Work: Don't Automate, Obliterate." In this article Hammer proposed what is now commonly referred to as "process reengineering." This topic is covered in detail later in this book.

The real irony is that information technology is one of the key enablers for dramatic process improvement. Advances in technology such as client-server computing, groupware, and handheld computers are enabling corporations to " . . . flatten organizations, yoke together teams across the barriers of specialty, rank and geography, and forge closer relationships with customers and suppliers."[8] As in these examples, the technology must support fundamental changes to the underlying processes and not simply be applied to the old, inefficient processes.

REORGANIZE

Companies spend enormous energy looking inward at organization, structure, and "spheres of influence," but practically none looking out at the customer and the marketplace. Consider what IBM Chairman Louis Gerstner Jr., says of his new company: "I have never seen a company so introspective, caught up in its own underwear, so preoccupied with internal processes . . . People in this company tell me it's easier doing business with people outside the company than inside."[9]

Companies often look solely to changes in reporting relationships to solve operating problems, as if there were a cause and effect relationship. Look at an organization chart — can you see process inefficiencies built in there? No, you have to look at a process map to see the inefficiencies. So why do we look to changes in the organization structure to solve process problems? One reason is that it is easy to do and it looks as if we are really doing something. Another reason is that there are truly some remarkable managers (even in a bureaucracy) who can get things done, and putting them in charge of problem areas often results in short-term improvements. Stories of "heroes" such as these can be found in almost every company. Unfortunately, you cannot rely on heroic efforts as an everyday way of running your business, or soon you won't have a business.

Reorganization can be a powerful tool for change when coupled with process improvements, but by itself it simply does not address the underlying problem of inefficient processes. One way in which reorganization is contributing to real performance improvement is when it is used to create "horizontal companies." This is a growing practice whereby employees are realigned from functional department "towers" to work on cross-functional teams organized around processes. Several leaders in the corporate world including AT&T, DuPont, General Electric, and Motorola are moving toward this model. Reorganizing around horizontal processes eliminates both hierarchy and functional department boundaries and creates an organization where virtually everyone works together in multidisciplinary teams that perform core processes.[10] The result? Streamlined, efficient business processes that place a priority on pleasing the customer rather than the boss.

> *I was to learn later in life that we tend to meet any new situation by reorganization . . . and a wonderful method it can be for creating the illusion of progress while producing confusion, inefficiency and demoralization.*
> —*Petronius Arbitor, 210 BC*

It should be clear by now that we need a new formula for responding to change. For twenty years, Total Quality Management (TQM) has been touted as the panacea for our performance problems. Organizational development advocates claim that the path to performance improvement is through our personnel. More recently, Business Process Reengineering has weighed in as the new champ on the block. Now we are hearing about the "learning organization" and the "virtual organization." Who is right? They all are.

Unfortunately, each of these excellent approaches is being characterized as being mutually exclusive. It is hard to find a process reengineering advocate who supports TQM, and the same is true in reverse. I believe this is a mistake. I advocate a synthesis of the best of each of these approaches. In the remaining chapters, I discuss in detail a methodology for managing change to deliver dramatic performance improvement — an approach that integrates the leading theories into a complete system of change called *Total Process Management*[SM] *(TPM)*.

PIECES OF THE PIE

3

Three Leading Change Management Approaches

All are but parts of one stupendous whole.

—Alexander Pope

There has always been a latest approach for managing organizational change, and the 1990s are no exception. In this chapter, the following three leading performance improvement approaches are discussed: Benchmarking, Total Quality Management, and Business Process Reengineering. For each I describe the approach and discuss its strengths and weaknesses. In Chapter Four, I introduce Total Process Management and explain how it incorporates each of these three approaches.

BENCHMARKING

Benchmarking is the process of comparing your organization and processes to world-class companies both within

Training Services

The MetaSys Change Management Group provides training and advisory services regarding change management to corporations world-wide. If you are interested in training or other information on the topics listed below, you can let us know in three convenient ways.

1) Simply complete this form and drop it in the mail, or
2) Fax this form to the following number: 214-994-6475, or
3) Call toll-free: 1-800-998-1981 and talk to a "real live" service representative.

Name _____ Title _____

Organization _____

Street Address _____

City / State (Country) _____ Zip _____

Telephone ( ) _____ Fax ( ) _____

Please send me more information on the following topics:

❑ Total Process Management ❑ Process Value Reinvention

❑ Process Mapping and Analysis Techniques ❑ Statistical Process Control

❑ Creating a Learning Organization ❑ Transforming Cultural Values

❑ Analytical Problem Solving Tools and Techniques ❑ Benchmarking

❑ Empowerment: Coaches and Self-directed teams ❑ ISO 9000

❑ Emerging Technologies as Change Enablers ❑ Process Value Improvement

and outside your industry. Benchmarking's purpose is to identify best-of-class business practices for goal setting and process improvement, and to identify your company's relative operating effectiveness and efficiency. Benchmarking looks beyond what results are achieved to the underlying business practices — to how the results are achieved.

Xerox initiated the rush to benchmarking with their pioneering efforts in the early 1980s. Because of the low retail prices of Japanese products, Xerox suspected them of dumping copiers in the United States to gain market share. Xerox decided to compare themselves to Japanese manufacturers through a process called "competitive benchmarking." The results were startling. They learned that the Japanese were so efficient that the Japanese product *retail* price was equivalent to the Xerox *manufacturing costs!*[1] Compared with Japanese manufacturers, Xerox had nine times as many production suppliers, and seven times as many manufacturing defects; product lead times were twice as long; and it took five times as long to set up a production line.[2]

> Benchmarking is the process of comparing your organization and processes to world-class companies both within and outside of your industry.

These initial benchmark results ushered in a new era at Xerox. By 1983, Xerox publicly committed to establishing leadership through quality, and benchmarking was a key tool used in the effort. Six years later their efforts were recognized when Xerox was awarded the prestigious Malcolm Baldrige National Quality Award. Today they are regarded as the world leaders in benchmarking.[3]

Benchmarking is relevant for processes throughout the company. It is not just for the key production processes

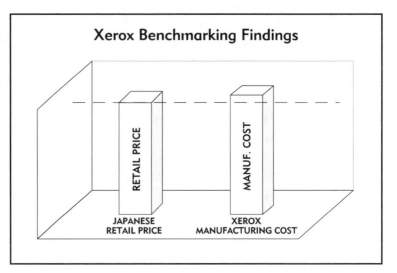

but also for service and "back-office" processes. At Xerox, benchmarking encompasses personnel, public relations, and even the cafeteria service.[4] Accounting is a frequently benchmarked function as is information services. Today, benchmark information is available for virtually any type of process.

A key mistake many companies make is to view benchmarking as a one-time event. Benchmarking must be continuous just as process improvement is continuous. Compaq, for instance, maintains a permanent research staff in a continuous effort to examine Compaq's 25 major competitors and to determine where they stand relative to particular processes.[5]

Benchmarking is often portrayed as a stand-alone change-management approach. Despite the successes noted earlier, benchmarking is rarely successful in delivering improvement results when employed by itself. Done poorly, benchmarking can be a waste of time that turns your team into nothing more than "industrial tourists."[6] In Total Process Management (TPM), benchmarking has an integral role, but it is viewed as only one part in a larger performance improvement framework. In TPM, benchmarking is used to provide ideas about ways in which to change processes and business practices that other companies have proven to be successful. It is also used to help companies understand their performance level compared to competitors.

However, there is no guarantee that methods which work for other companies will work for yours. The director of product marketing, Xerox Computer Services, shared the following experience:

> *Do competitive benchmarking, but be careful; your objective is to satisfy your customer's needs, not match or exceed your competitor's products. Remember, they may have fallen into some classical traps as well. In some cases they fall short of, in other cases they exceed requirements. Your most important input comes from existing or prospective customers.[7]*

The practices other companies employ may be better than yours, but they may not be the best possible — potentially your company could conceive of ways of conducting business not thought of before. That is the real path to competitive strength. No company can ever hope to achieve significant competitive strength by only doing what the competition is already doing. The CEO of one company in a highly competitive industry confessed to me his frustration with his company's lack of success in keeping up with their leading competitor. He said, "We do everything they do, but by the time we start to be good at it, they come out with something new. We're tired of getting our butts kicked, but they always seem to be a step ahead of us." I expected his next comment to be, "It's just

No company can ever hope to achieve significant competitive strength by only doing what the competition is already doing.

not fair . . ." No, competition isn't fair, and you won't win by trying to imitate your competitors. C.K. Prahalad supports this with the following statement:

> *Imitation may be the sincerest form of flattery, but it will not lead to competitive revitalization. Strategies based on imitation are transparent to competitors who have already mastered them. Moreover, successful companies rarely stand still. So it is not surprising that many executives feel trapped in a seemingly endless game of catch-up — regularly surprised by the new accomplishments of their rivals.*[8]

Benchmarking can be useful, but it is no substitute for innovation. Total Process Management uses benchmarking as a source of ideas, but it emphasizes innovation through creative brainstorming. Although one entire part of the TPM methodology is dedicated to benchmarking (Part 4, Conduct Benchmarking), a separate section is dedicated to innovation (Part 6, Brainstorm Innovations).

TOTAL QUALITY MANAGEMENT

Around two decades ago, America realized that something remarkable happened in Japan during the post-war reconstruction. While American businesses were happily raking in profits during the booming, post-war years, the Japanese were listening to an American—W. Edwards Deming. His message: Build quality into the fabric of your company.

Slow and steady wins the race.
—Aesop

The Japanese perfected the application of the idea of *kaizen* (Figure 3.2) which means gradual continuous improvement. Through the international application of this idea the Japanese achieved remarkable competitive success. Since the wake-up call of Japan's competitive message, American companies have embraced quality as essential to their success. Today, quality is no longer a competitive advantage; rather, it is a barrier to entry. "If you can't meet a world standard of quality at the world's best price, you're not even in the game."[9] Many American companies now compete for the prestigious Malcolm Baldrige National Quality Award (see Appendix A), and companies in the international community are committing to achieve ISO 9000 quality system certification (see Appendix B) in unprecedented numbers.

Controversy rages as to the definition of quality. The three leaders of the quality movement, W. Edwards Deming, Philip B. Crosby, and J.M. Juran, disagree on many points; however, two things they agree on are customer focus and the requirement for continuous improvement. The focus of quality is to identify and exceed cus-

The focus of quality is to identify and exceed customer expectations for service and product performance.

tomer expectations for service and product performance. The elements of TQM include focus on the customer, employee involvement and teamwork, benchmarking, and continuous improvement.

When implemented properly, quality is *not* a program. Quality is a mindset. TQM is predicated on internalizing quality as a corporate value, and in creating a "quality culture." Studies indicate that as much as 70% or more of quality efforts fail to deliver the expected results.[10] Much of this relates to lack of corporate and executive emphasis on the value of quality.[11] A quality culture is a deliberately selected and constructed way of life. It requires that quality be incorporated into every aspect of an organization. In the fall of 1993, General Motors demonstrated the real meaning of commitment to quality. GM was faced with compromising their quality standards by shipping sub-par automobiles, or adhering to their quality standards and losing approximately $1 billion in sales. As hard as the decision must have been, GM stuck to the quality standards and gave up the sales.[12] If more companies took this attitude, undoubtedly there would be far fewer TQM "failures."

Total Quality Management has its roots in manufacturing companies. In America, TQM was perceived as essential to balancing the competitive scales with the Japanese manufacturers who had long since mastered creating quality products at a low cost. Even in companies implementing TQM, it was relegated principally to departments related to manufacturing. The association with manufacturing explains in part why TQM has achieved only limited acceptance in the service sector. For instance, only three companies in the history of the Malcolm Baldrige National Quality Award have been in the service category.

The association with manufacturing explains in part why TQM has achieved only limited acceptance in the service sector.

Recently, the term *quality* has taken on a negative connotation for companies trying to implement continuous improvement. Some companies see the link with manufacturing as a barrier to acceptance throughout the organization. For this reason, Rubbermaid renamed TQM in their company to "Continuous Value Improvement." The CEO of Rubbermaid said, "The term 'total quality' can be con-

Figure 3.3

Through 1993,
service compa-
nies comprise
only 15% of the
Malcolm Baldrige
National Quality
Award winners.

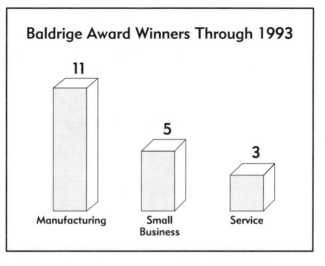

Baldrige Award Winners Through 1993

11	5	3
Manufacturing	Small Business	Service

fined to manufacturing. We wanted to take it across the business."[13]

Another reason for TQM's negative reputation is the perception that it provides a one-dimensional solution. Companies are wanting to emphasize other attributes of performance, such as cost, service, speed, and innovation. Some people worry that obsessing about quality alone can cause companies to lose sight of the bigger picture, like what your customers might want in product innovations.[14] "Quality programs, with their single-minded championing of things like zero defects, for instance, are especially prone to tunnel vision and navel gazing."[15] Georg Becker, CFO of Germany-based Mueller Chemical Company, believes that his company's focus on TQM contributed to conditions that led to the need for layoffs and corporate downsizing. He states the following:

With TQM, I admit that a lot of change for the better occurred, but the distractions that came with the program have taken us away from our company's original goal—to be the chemicals market leader in Europe. While we spent our time organizing teams, de-

veloping measurement systems, and filling out week-
ly quality reports, our competition concentrated on
sales and took away much of the European market share
we had planned for ourselves.[16]

The advantages of TQM are that it involves everyone in the organization, achieves improvement in small manageable chunks, and promotes "raising the bar" to new levels of performance excellence. The grass-roots implementation element of TQM has a distinct advantage over focused, project team, and top-down approaches to performance improvement. TQM harnesses the minds of *everyone* in the company to think of ways to improve performance. The collective contribution of thousands of frontline employees far outstrips the capacity of the relatively fewer numbers of management employees. Also, change under TQM can be more acceptable to organizations because it introduces improvements incrementally. Employees have longer to adapt to changes and the magnitude of change is relatively small (compared to Business Process Reengineering).

Total Quality Management has several significant drawbacks that have contributed to its fall from grace. Some of these are discussed on the next pages.

TQM: Slow Results

Because TQM usually takes several years to achieve substantial improvements, companies in dire competitive straits may not have time to wait. By the time these companies begin to see process improvements, they have already been run out of business. These companies need a tool that provides immediate and dramatic improvement. One CEO explains his choice of Business Process Reengineering over TQM by saying, "Our markets were moving too fast for incremental change to work. We had to get people on board."[17]

Western societies do not value long-term improvement in the way that the Japanese society does. Wall Street looks for results every *three months* — Japanese executives think in terms of *many years* to achieve their goals. In the West, it is difficult to put off results today to reap greater benefits in the future. Executives taking this approach often find themselves typing up their resumes. It is no surprise then that TQM is a particularly difficult pill to swallow for most western executives needing quick results.

TQM is a difficult pill to swallow for executives needing quick results.

TQM: Significant Investment

Many companies cannot see past the initial startup cost to the benefits available from improved performance. Companies that start down a TQM path frequently give it up when expenses outweigh the gains for too long a time. TQM requires significant outlays for product testing, quality audits, preventive maintenance, and employee training. What executives don't see are the much higher costs of low quality that show up as scrap, rework, lost sales, and returns. The real cost of poor quality is much higher than that of TQM — at times as much as 500% or more. Unfortunately, this just doesn't mean much to executives having cash flow or profitability problems and facing angry stockholders.

TQM: Long-term Executive Support

Turnover at the top of a company can result in new management that does not value TQM. In the West, most top executives rarely stay in their positions more than a couple of years. Without executive support, TQM can exist only in isolated cells and will not deliver significant results. One reason for the recent love affair with Business Process Reengineering (BPR) is that it delivers significant returns in a relatively short time. Executives can sponsor a BPR project, see results within two years, and leave with a positive track record (even if the results aren't sustainable in the long run)!

TQM: Narrow Focus

The association of TQM with manufacturing, a significant contributor to the view that TQM has a narrow focus, was discussed in detail earlier in this chapter. Another contributor to the view that TQM is too narrow is that improvement is usually limited to a single department, and related activities outside the department often are not addressed. This can lead to making a sub-process more efficient at the expense of making the overall process less efficient.

An international company with over 2,000 retail outlets made this mistake and learned how costly sub-optimization can be. I was in the middle of evaluating their "goods and services acquisition" process when I learned of a process improvement idea that went wrong. The process in question cut across the merchandising, purchasing, receiving, and accounts payable departments. One department decided that the practice of centrally issuing one purchase order to a vendor was too restrictive on the stores. That department implemented a practice where stores issued their own purchase orders. This was a great idea and it worked well — for the stores. Nobody bothered to look further down the process to the effect on accounts payable. The results were disastrous. Instead of getting one invoice, accounts payable suddenly started receiving thousands more each month. This caused the impact on personnel costs to more than offset the gains in store buying flexibility.

A third contributor to the narrow scope view is that TQM does not challenge the viability of the work itself. Instead of asking how to improve a certain activity, the question should be does it need to be done at all? The advantage of Business Process Reengineering is that it starts with a blank page — novel solutions may require that entire non-value added activities be omitted.[18]

BUSINESS PROCESS REENGINEERING

Why take a "slow boat to China" when you can take a supersonic jet? That is the idea behind business process

We haven't the time to take our time.

— Eugène Ionesco

reengineering. Probably no business management philosophy has gained such widespread popularity and media attention in such a short time as business process reengineering. It is difficult to pick up a business magazine today that doesn't mention reengineering somewhere. The remarkable thing is that the term "reengineering" was coined less than four years ago.

Michael Hammer introduced the idea of reengineering in a pivotal article in the *Harvard Business Review* (July-August, 1990). Hammer will tell you that he didn't invent reengineering. He simply put together existing ideas into a novel approach. The fundamental difference in Hammer's message is the degree of draconian change necessary for dramatic performance improvement. Where others emphasize improving what exists, Hammer advocates a wrecking ball approach: As he says, "At the heart of reengineering is the notion of discontinuous thinking — of recognizing and breaking away from the outdated rules and fundamental assumptions that underlie operations."[19] In his follow-up book, *Reengineering the Corporation,* Hammer offers the following formal definition of reengineering: "The fundamental rethinking and radical redesign of business processes to achieve dramatic improvements in critical, contemporary measures of performance, such as cost, quality, service, and speed."

> *Reengineering is the fundamental rethinking and radical redesign of business processes to achieve dramatic improvements in critical, contemporary measures of performance, such as cost, quality, service, and speed.*
> — *Michael Hammer*

Why the love affair with reengineering? The application of reengineering can produce astonishing results. For example, cycle times can be reduced from months to days, costs can be reduced by 40% and up, and productivity and quality can be improved by 1000% or more.

Why do we need *dramatic* change; why can't we just settle for incremental improvement instead? Isn't radical change destructive to the organization? Yes, BPR is a painful and wrenching experience, but for many companies the pain of radical change is worth it. Many companies have little choice. Clearly BPR can deliver substantial competitive advantage, or restore a poorly performing company to competitive health. This is an extremely compelling argument for executives surrounded by fierce competitors, dissatisfied shareholders, and uncompromising boards of directors. Here is a tool that quickly delivers big results.

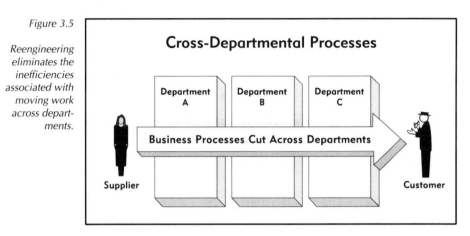

One of the reasons dramatic improvements are possible through reengineering is that BPR focuses on processes, and not on departments. Departments are functional towers of expertise — processes are the system of activities that collectively create value for customers. Reengineering looks at improving overall process performance without regard to departments. This eliminates the hand-offs, redundant activities, and other inefficiencies associated with moving work across departments. Cross-departmental process reengineering infringes on turf in a *big way*. Turf infringement is one of the leading reasons for the organizational resistance that reengineering faces.

Another characteristic of reengineering is that it generally is conducted on a very large scale on unique projects that isolate specific processes for improvement. These projects can be concluded in a relatively short time (from several months to a year), although implementation of the improvements may take longer.

Business process reengineering looks at processes from the perspective of the customer. In BPR, each activity is evaluated and classified as to adding value or not adding value to the customer. The criterion is simple. If the customer would pay you to do it, it adds value; otherwise it adds cost. The average ratio of value-added to non-value-added activity is a startling 5%![20] In my experience, it is rarely over one percent. That means that as much as 95% to 99% of our work does not add value to the customer!

Figure 3.6

On average, an astounding 95% of activities do not add value from the customer's perspective.

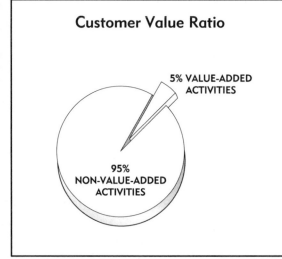

Customer Value Ratio

5% VALUE-ADDED ACTIVITIES

95% NON-VALUE-ADDED ACTIVITIES

The non-value-added activities are the target of process reengineering improvements and the reason that process reengineering is an essential component of Total Process Management. With such an enormous percentage of the work not contributing to what the customer wants, how can companies hope to "incrementalize" their way to efficiency? More often than not, they can't. Problems this large require improvement in big

If the customer would pay you to do it, it adds value; otherwise it just adds cost.

chunks and companies hope to achieve these improvements with BPR.

Is reengineering really one big honeymoon? Hardly. Granted, BPR can deliver remarkable short-term improvements in the processes selected for reengineering. However, there is little evidence that the improvements are sustainable and that major process improvements translate into a significant impact on the bottom line. One consultant explains, "There were truly dramatic impacts on processes — 60% to 80% reductions in cost and cycle time — but only very modest effects at the business unit level, because the changes didn't matter in terms of the customer."[21] A recent article in the *Harvard Business Review* states the following:

> *In all too many companies, reengineering has been not only a great success, but also a great failure. After months, even years, of careful redesign, these companies achieve dramatic improvements in individual processes only to watch overall results decline. By now, paradoxical outcomes such as this have become almost commonplace.*[22]

The remarkable improvements available through business process reengineering may seem too good to be true. The doubters are becoming increasingly vocal. The Director of the Center for Technology and Productivity for the Columbia School of Business writes in the Readers Report section of *Business Week* (July 5, 1993):

> *Reengineering, although currently in vogue, is certainly not new, and it has yet to be convincingly demonstrated that it yields predictably positive results. Little is known about how one successfully reengineers a business and even less about how one measures the return on investment in this type of investment, in spite of what many consultants say.*

There is also the perplexing question of how you do reengineering. After I gave a speech in Boston about process reengineering, an audience member said to me, "I've read all the books, Hammer, Harrington, and others. I am convinced that we should be doing reengineering, but nobody provides useful instructions on how you do reengineering. Where do I go to find out?" (This book!)

There is woefully little agreement on what reengineering is. Almost every company and consultant claims to be doing reengineering. Often these people are simply implementing a new information system, restructuring to reduce headcount, or centralizing/decentralizing operations, and calling it "reengineering." These sound more like the traditional approaches discussed and dismissed as ineffective in Chapter 2, Birth of the Chocolate Elephant. Due to the lack of clear understanding of what reengineering is, many companies (and consultants) are packaging traditional, ineffective solutions as reengineering. Total Process Management avoids this pitfall by providing a clear definition and detailed steps on how to implement the methodology.

> Reengineering is so hot that the label is being slapped on everything from requests for new chairs to across-the-board layoffs.[23]

There are several significant disadvantages to Business Process Reengineering. The impact on the organization can be agonizing, companies view BPR as a one-time solution, and BPR is applied narrowly.

BPR: Agonizingly Tough

Although the results from reengineering can be significant, the toll it takes on an organization can't be overemphasized. "All change is a struggle. Dramatic across-the-company change is a war."[24] The CEO of Blue Cross of

Washington and Alaska raised claims processing productivity 20% in 15 months through reengineering. She says of the effort, "It was more difficult than anything we ever imagined, but it was worth it."[25]

BPR introduces dramatic and sudden change that virtually *shocks* the organization. Departments are combined or wiped out entirely. Jobs are lost or are irrevocably changed. Management jobs are eliminated or transformed into coaching and advisory roles. Employees are suddenly asked to assume new responsibility and authority — some for the first time in their lives. Ultimately, every worker asks: "What happens to me?"

All change is a struggle. Dramatic across-the-company change is war.[24]

Except in rare circumstances, reengineering leads to a reduction in jobs. During a year of *record earnings*, William Weiss, CEO of Ameritech, announced a seven percent cut in jobs. He said the following:

> *You can't keep people from feeling scared. I doubt the downsizing is over. But my view is that every aspect of life has its uncertainties. Everyone knows this business is going through a transformation. There's no way that you can give people assurance other than what they can earn in the marketplace.*[26]

As in the Ameritech example, job loss has become increasingly common even in healthy companies. Unlike layoffs, BPR eliminates or changes the underlying activities, but the result is the same — with less work to do, companies need fewer workers. One estimate calls for as many as 25 million jobs (out of approximately 90 million jobs) to be lost in the private sector.[27] In executing BPR, companies must recognize and acknowledge employee fears of losing their jobs. If not dealt with effectively, employee fears can ultimately sabotage the change effort.

BPR: One-time Effort

A second disadvantage is that reengineering is often seen as a one-time shot. The gains through BPR are not consolidated and enhanced. Almost immediately after implementation, the benefits begin to erode and this continues at an increasing pace until the positive effects are negligible. The chart shown in Figure 3.7 illustrates the effect of BPR without the benefit of continuous process improvement.

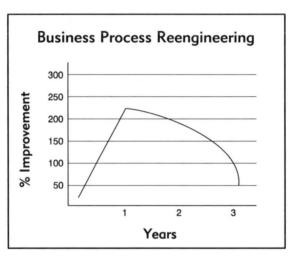

Most people view reengineering and continuous improvement approaches such as Total Quality Management as being mutually exclusive. In *Reengineering the Corporation*, Michael Hammer, reengineering's most prominent advocate, dedicates only a half page to continuous improvement—and then only to explain the difference between it and reengineering.[28]

Companies that tried and gave up on TQM or that don't see it as a fit for their organization readily embrace reengineering. Conversely, companies with a strong quality culture just don't see the need for reengineering. For example, the reengineering manager for a 12,000 employee financial services firm told me that most divisions were doing reengineering but only one division had implemented TQM. Despite the reengineering successes in other divisions, the TQM manager would not consider also conducting reengineering projects. His excuse was that TQM and reengineering are the same thing. (They're not.)

Many people view process reengineering and Total Quality Management as being mutually exclusive.

There are some people who view the combination of reengineering and continuous improvement as not just complementary, but as essential. One management consultant said, "You can't do reengineering without an environment of continuous improvement or TQM." He continued by saying that without the supporting elements of continuous improvement such as worker involvement and training "painfully won gains will leak away."[29] Even Michael Hammer, while ever true to the reengineering message, acknowledges that reengineering and quality programs are complementary under a process management umbrella.[30]

> *Continuous improvement is an essential tool for consolidating and propagating gains from performance improvements. Reducing bureaucracy (a major source of inefficiency) and keeping it down is often not as easy as it seems — powerful forces are at work within organizations to regress to inefficient ways of doing things. Bureaucracy "becomes like a cancer that must be attacked vigorously, systematically and with determination."[31]*

Arguably the greatest characteristic of Total Process Management is that it brings together, under a single methodology, reengineering and continuous improvement. TPM recognizes that one without the other is only half of the solution. Reengineering without continuous improvement delivers dramatic improvements only to see them "leak away." Continuous improvement without reengineering may not deliver results fast enough to save the company. TPM provides the answer—a holistic solution in which reengineering and continuous improvement are synthesized into a single methodology.

> *Arguably the greatest characteristic of Total Process Management is that it brings together, under a single methodology, reengineering and continuous improvement.*

BPR: Applied Narrowly

Another disadvantage is that only the few people who work on BPR projects learn anything about how process reengineering works, and how it can be implemented throughout the organization. There is little or no institutional learning about the process of conducting BPR. How will the improvements be sustained and propagated under these circumstances? Business process reengineering is usually focused on a few key processes. This narrow focus creates an additional problem. How is the remainder of the organization to improve the speed, cost, and quality of their processes if only a few will benefit from BPR?

The obvious answer is to combine reengineering with continuous improvement. With Total Process Management, organizations are able to achieve cycles of sustained improvement interrupted by periods of rapid, dramatic improvement. (The chart in Figure 3.8 illustrates this relationship.) Through TPM, the narrow focus of

Figure 3.8

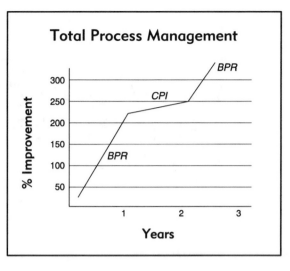

reengineering is offset through teaching the same underlying principles and techniques throughout the organization to be applied continuously to processes at all levels. In this way, companies can take advantage of the short-term, high-impact benefits of reengineering, and at the same time achieve long-term sustained improvement broadly across the organization.

EATING THE CHOCOLATE ELEPHANT

An Introduction to Total Process Management

"New things are made familiar, and familiar things are made new."

—*Samuel Johnson*

Total Process Management (TPM) is a performance improvement methodology that starts with corporate mission and strategy and embraces both discontinuous, dramatic change and continuous, incremental improvement. Also, it addresses all four organizational levers for change: process, systems, structure, and people. The primary difference between TPM and the other leading theories is that it is a *complete* approach for implementing organizational change to *achieve and sustain tangible bottom-line performance improvement.*

Total Process Management is represented in Figure 4.1 as a "constellation" of interrelated elements. At the center of the constellation is the customer. Everything in TPM revolves around satisfying the customer. At the top is mission and strategy — these provide the framework that focuses everyone in the organization around a common purpose. At opposite ends of the change continuum are process value improvement and process value reinvention. Benchmarking is shared between them as an essential tool for establishing external focus. Within the constellation are the four organizational levers for change: process, systems, structure, and people. Together, these elements provide a complete framework for managing change and improving performance — Total Process Management.

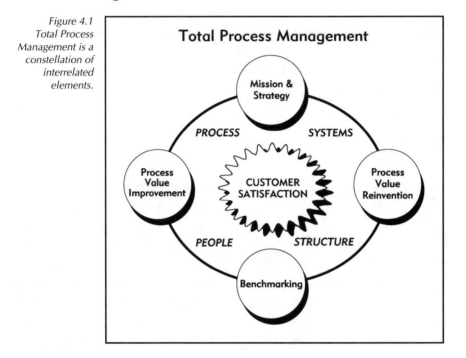

Figure 4.1
Total Process
Management is a
constellation of
interrelated
elements.

CUSTOMER SATISFACTION

Plenty is being written about focusing on the customer. However, with a few notable exceptions, very few companies are consistently *achieving* customer satisfaction. All processes are defined by inputs, processing, and output. Traditionally, the customer became involved at the point of output, when companies used legions of salespeople and marketing acumen to convince buyers that they needed the offered product. That worked fine for a while. However, since the 1970s, competition has intensified in virtually every arena. In today's markets, companies must be pin-point precise in understanding and meeting customer expectations to stay competitive. That means asking customers for information about the process, involving them during the process, and asking for comments on the output.

Some companies are recognizing that customer focus is more than just conducting surveys and providing response cards along with their products. Smart companies are recognizing that customer expectations should drive *fundamental business structure.* "The way to win is to reexamine every cherished assumption and redesign entire organizations around customer needs."[1] For instance, General Motors is rethinking the way it divides the car market. After nearly a million customer interviews, GM realized that their old view of the market was not in sync with customer views. Historically, GM looked at cars on a continuum. That continuum was from small to big and from cheap to expensive. Now it is designing specific models for specific consumer segments based on age, income, and lifestyle needs.[2] The following is an example from another company.

> お客様は神様です
>
> *Okyakusama wa kamisama desu.*
> — *"The Customer is God."*

> After taking over as CEO at Micrografx (an international software development company), Gordon Tucker spent three months interviewing customers and evaluating product effectiveness. At the end of that time he spearheaded a fundamental restructuring of the business based on customer comments.

The old structure left product design in the hands of the software engineers. This resulted in "inside-out" design of the products. Whatever new technology came along went into the product, whether the customer wanted it or not. The new structure is organized around customer markets. Cross-functional product teams (led by "customer category managers" and including customers, software engineers, salespersons, and others) define product specifications using "outside-in" design. Tucker is counting on the new structure to drive product design that goes beyond satisfaction, to surprise and delight Micrografx customers.

Customer-focused companies recognize that customers' perceptions are shaped by every contact they have with the company — not just by use of the product. These companies drive customer focus into every corner of the business. The CFO of Dell Computer said in a speech that the people at Dell are no more than two levels away from the customer. They either interact directly with the customer or they support the people who interact directly with the customer. The following is an example of how even corporate service departments can focus on external customers.

Accounts receivable (AR) is a function that typically views itself as a corporate watchdog responsible for bringing non-paying customers to bay. Like most accounting functions, it is designed to serve the needs of the company (internal focus), not the customer. True, AR has an important fiduciary responsibility to the company. How might the people in AR have an *external focus* that showed concern for the customer? One company asked their customers and found that many of them couldn't understand the bill, and thought it was inaccurate. The bill had been designed for the convenience of the accounts receivable department, in disregard for the customer.[3] This accounts receivable department has the opportunity to both serve the customer and to reduce outstanding receivables simply by being customer-focused.

As obvious as it may seem, the point still must be made — customer focus cannot occur in inwardly focused companies. Successful companies must make the *customer* boss. Traditionally, doing the job well and satisfying the boss have been the prerequisites for success. This often puts employees in the position of having to choose between what they *ought to do* (to satisfy the customer) and what the *job calls for them to do* (which satisfies the boss).[4] Companies cannot hope to achieve customer focus so long as they maintain a hierarchical command and control management structure (which makes managers responsible to each other instead of to the customer).[5] Departments don't deliver value to customers, processes do. It is only when companies organize around process, with customer-driven performance goals, that they can truly become customer focused.

Departments don't deliver value to customers, processes do.

Total Process Management puts customer satisfaction at the heart of performance improvement. Through TPM, companies can see how to flatten the hierarchy and organize multi-functional teams around processes to increase value for the customer. With company-wide process improvement, *every* function is encouraged to focus on customer requirements, not just core processes.

MISSION AND STRATEGY

The remainder of this book describes how to achieve performance excellence. However, performance excellence is predicated on a company already having an effective mission and strategy. That is a big assumption. Mission is what defines the purpose of an organization. Without it there is no clear understanding of where the company is going — employees do not know the context in which to make decisions. I commented to one CEO who initiated a corporate turnaround that the company's mission no longer seemed to fit the direction he was taking the company. His response was, "Yeah, I guess we should change the mission statement." And that is where it stands to this day. Here was a CEO who was restructuring, laying off employees, and asking the company to be "customer focused," who had not even established what *business* to be customer-focused in.

An effective mission statement says where a company is going, and "provides a noble cause" for people. A good mission statement can't be outgrown. NASA had the mission to put a man on the moon. When that was done, they struggled for a purpose — "What now?" A good mission evolves over time. As the business environment changes, so must a company's purpose. Imagine the company well established as the leading maker of buggy whips when the automobile came along. How useful to them was their mission? The statement below, for Stephen Covey's Institute for Principle-Centered Leadership, is an example of a good mission statement.

> *If you don't know where you're going, you will probably end up somewhere else.*
> — Laurence Johnston Peter

> *Our mission is to empower people and organizations to significantly increase their performance capability in order to achieve worthwhile purposes through understanding and living principle-centered leadership.*[6]

An effective strategy is equally important. If mission says where we are going, strategy says how we will get there. The traditional approach to strategy places dominating existing product segments as the central concern. The assumption is that dominant products make companies great. If this were true, what has happened to General Motors, for years the dominant car maker in the industry but now in a furious state of "catch-up" with thriving competitors? What about Xerox? How did the company that *invented* xerography ever lose half their market share to Canon in key markets?[7] Ultimately, customers define what has value, and only processes *deliver* value. Successful companies are recognizing that great processes make great products, and subsequently, great companies. It is essential that corporate leaders include process excellence in corporate strategy. "Every company has business processes that deliver value to the customer. But few think of them as the primary object of strategy."[8]

There are almost as many approaches to strategy as there are consultants. From "core competencies" to "globalization," there are almost unlimited ideas about strategy, and most of them are good ones. My purpose here is not to stake out an exclusive approach to corporate strategy. Rather, it is to emphasize the role of process in an effective corporate strategy. "The building blocks of corporate strategy are not products and markets but business processes. Competitive success depends on transforming a company's key processes into strategic capabilities that consistently provide superior value to the customer."[9] Lawrence Bossidy, CEO at AlliedSignal, said, "The competitive difference is not in deciding what to do, but in how to do it. Execution becomes paramount."[10]

For these reasons, I advocate including Total Process Management as an integral component of corporate strategy. Good products don't make winners, but winners make good products. TPM provides the mechanism for creating world-class, customer-focused processes. Focusing on processes allows you the flexibility to adapt to changing market needs and opportunities, which is a prerequisite for competitive success.

INCREASING VALUE-ADDED TO THE CUSTOMER: PROCESS IMPROVEMENT AND REINVENTION

All along, we have used the terms Business Process Reengineering (BPR) and Total Quality Management (TQM) — why the switch to *process value reinvention (PVR)* and *process value improvement (PVI)*? Both Business Process Reengineering and Total Quality Management are existing methodologies with widespread connotations as to their composition and application. Each has its respective positive and negative baggage. I want to avoid associations with the existing methodologies — Total Process Management, while predicated on common techniques and elements, is a unique approach. Associations with other approaches will only lead to confusion and unfounded biases.

> *Total Process Management, while predicated on common techniques and elements, is a unique approach.*

The names *process value improvement* and *process value reinvention* differ from Total Quality Management and Business Process Reengineering to reflect the underlying philosophy of Total Process Management. Performance improvement is predicated on increasing the *value* being added for customers. Only processes deliver value — hence the first two words: "process value." (For brevity's sake, the word "value" is sometimes omitted, for example, "process reinvention," but the meaning is the same.) Also, Total Process Management views process reinvention and process improvement as the *same in method, but differing in scope and how they are applied.* Process reinvention is done at the macro-level by project teams working on a short timeframe. Process improvement uses the same principles and techniques as process reinvention, but is done broadly across the corporation, at a micro-level by the workgroups themselves.

Another reason for the different names is to further distinguish process value improvement and reinvention from other approaches. Process improvement is substantively different from TQM in several ways. Unlike TQM, process value improvement stresses improvement across the *entire* range of performance drivers: cycle time, efficiency, *and* quality. Process improvement is not only for manufacturing — it is for every industry. With process improvement, there is no need to wait on institutionalizing performance improvement for benefits to accrue — anyone with initiative can apply the techniques immediately.

Likewise, process value reinvention is deliberately different from reengineering. The term reengineering carries with it a technical connotation that implies that it is not for everyone, only a highly trained few. It also implies (along with explicit reinforcement by reengineering leaders such as Michael Hammer and Thomas H. Davenport) that process reengineering is primarily an exercise in system development and automation. Granted, technology can be a significant enabler to dramatic improvement, but it is hardly a prerequisite. I have seen remarkable results with virtually no automation, through just applying the performance improvement principles. Ultimately, our goal is to start over with our processes without preconceived notions, to *reinvent* our business. In addition, we want to reinvent our processes along all of the key dimensions: process, structure, people, *and* systems.

By themselves, Business Process Reengineering and Total Quality Management are incomplete solutions.

The last reason is that *everyone* can participate in process reinvention. The principles and techniques are the same as those used in process improvement, but you just apply them differently.

By themselves, business process reengineering and Total Quality Management are incomplete solutions. There simply is no mechanism in TQM for achieving rapid, dramatic performance improvement across organizational boundaries. Reengineering does not offer any way to institutionalize continuous improvement across an organization to sustain and enhance performance improvements. As shown in the chart in Figure 4.2, Total Process Management brings together the divergent characteristics of these two approaches to capitalize on the strengths of each.

Total Process Management does more than just add reengineering and Total Quality Management together and call it by a different name. If you only place reengineering on top of TQM, you will achieve an "oil and water" effect—they won't mix, but rather will exist as "separate but equal" methodologies. There will be no common language or understanding of the shared characteristics of each. Simply combining them is not enough to generate true synergy.

In TPM, process reinvention and improvement are seen as essentially the same in method but differing in scope.

In TPM, process reinvention and improvement are seen as essentially the same in method but differing in scope.

There are seven parts in the TPM methodology; the first two parts comprise the foundation for performance improvement, and the final five parts constitute the performance improvement cycle. These seven elements are equally applicable for both process reinvention and improvement. The TPM methodology is depicted in Figure 4.3.

Figure 4.2

TPM brings
the divergent
characteristics of
Total Quality
Management
and process
reengineering
together to
capitalize on
the strengths
of each.

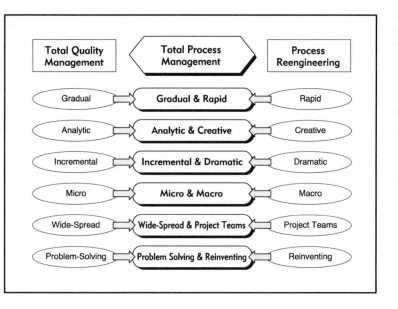

Both process value improvement and reinvention require organizational commitment, beginning at the executive level. The techniques to improve processes and organizational performance are the same for both. For each, you must understand the current environment, research best practices and competitor performance, understand customer requirements, set stretch performance targets, generate innovations, and implement the new ideas.

Process value improvement and reinvention exist at opposite ends of the "change continuum." Viewing them in this manner creates the flexibility to pick the point or multiple points along the continuum that are best suited for the unique circumstances in which your company finds itself. For example, a healthy company may choose to implement the process improvement component of TPM and reinvent key processes on a just-in-time basis. Another company may respond to a competitive threat by conducting process reinvention for a key process, and follow it with a roll-out of company-wide process improvement starting with the reinvented process. Because the under-

Figure 4.3

The seven-part
Total Process
Management
methodology
is the same for
both process
improvement and
for process
reinvention.

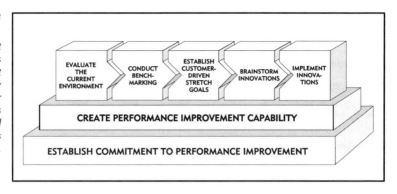

lying methodology is the same for both PVI and PVR, there is no wasted motion or training in shifting emphasis from one to the other in response to changing business conditions.

So how are process value reinvention and process improvement different? Make no mistake, these two are *very different*, but not in technique — only in how the technique is *applied*.

Process value improvement seeks performance gains at the lowest level. Sponsorship of change is at the workgroup level, and so rarely results in rapid and dramatic change across the organization. PVI takes time — a lot more time than process reinvention. Mobilizing an entire organization and institutionalizing the required skills and mindset is a lengthy process — period.

In contrast, process reinvention generally targets processes that cut broadly across the organization and are seen as strategic to the organization — processes that are sometimes referred to as "value chains." Also, PVR is done *fast*, usually through an independent project team that transcends the departments that contribute to the targeted process.

Figure 4.4

Process improvement and reinvention are the same in method, but differ in scope.

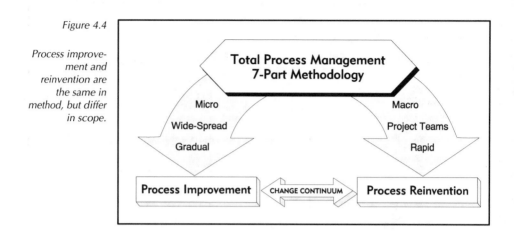

Despite these tangible differences, the tools and techniques for process reinvention and process improvement are the same. The graphic in Figure 4.4 illustrates the relationship.

BENCHMARKING

In Total Process Management, benchmarking is viewed as a tool, equally appropriate for process value improvement and reinvention, for gaining insights into world-class practices and for building consensus for the need to change. After all, it is a hollow argument to say that certain performance levels are impossible when someone else is already achieving them. However, benchmarking plays another role in TPM — that of creating external focus as a cultural value.

Benchmarking provides insights into world-class practices and builds consensus for the need to change.

Benchmarking is a primary mechanism for promoting an externally focused organization. Internal focus is one of the chief contributors to business performance decline. Companies that insist that their way is the best and only way create a deadly spiral in which inbred solutions and ways of thinking create an ever-increasing competitive disadvantage. These companies are unlikely to participate in benchmarking and rarely act on the information when they do benchmark. An extreme case of inward focus is illustrated below.

> A seven billion dollar international retailer had a policy of hiring from outside the company for only entry-level positions, never at the top or middle management levels. This policy perpetuated outdated business practices and processes. I conducted an extensive benchmarking exercise as part of a larger reengineering effort, after which they were astonished to find that their corporate performance ranked last in virtually every category benchmarked. At times they were worse by a factor of 200% or more! The organization denied the results and found limitless justifications for "being different." If your business is different enough, you can make a case that the benchmark results aren't comparing the same things. Business process reengineering recommendations from this study could have led to $50 million in annual savings. Still the organization struggled against the recommendations. They simply could not face changing their age-old culture and business practices. Their extreme inward focus denied the reality of the marketplace. A year later, little or no progress had been made in implementing the recommendations, and the company continues to lag far behind the competition.

In recognizing benchmarking's importance to performance excellence, Total Process Management dedicates an entire part of the methodology to benchmarking.

ORGANIZATIONAL LEVERS FOR CHANGE

Change does not happen because someone decrees that it should — although some CEOs have tried! Change is dif-ficult, and it will be resisted. Transforming business policies and practices is something that must be entered into deliberate-ly and with full commitment from the executive team. Orga-nizations and people change when the supporting envi-ronment changes. In Total Process Management, there are four organizational levers for implementing change: pro-cess, systems, structure, and people.

Change the environment; do not try to change man.
— Richard Buckminster Fuller

Figure 4.5

All four organiza-tional levers for change must be addressed.

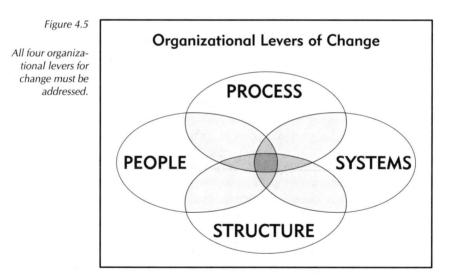

Process

People in different functional departments hate each oth-er. They do not cooperate, do not trust each other, do not have common goals, and do not focus on the customer.

Even in a cooperative environment, it is all but impossible to have efficient processes across departments. There are invariably too many hand-offs where errors, redundancies, and other inefficiencies can occur. For instance, Ryder Systems reported that before adopting a process focus, buying a vehicle for leasing required from *fourteen to seventeen hand-offs*.[11] Similarly, Bell Atlantic Corporation found that an order for telephone lines "passed through 28 hands before the order was filled. All those steps added costs, slowed the order down and introduced opportunity for error."[12] However, as the following quote indicates, times are changing.

> *"There is nearly unanimous opinion forming that in the 1990s we'll be running businesses primarily by customer-oriented processes. We're breaking down the walls that separate finance and manufacturing and engineering and marketing, and putting all these functional disciplines into process organizations.*[13]

Companies are shifting to a new management model — "the horizontal corporation." In this model, "It's about managing across, not up."[14] Companies identify their key processes, assign "process owners," align employees from multiple functions into teams, and assign them responsibility for satisfying customer expectations. This arrangement "takes an organization's focus off its own internal structure and puts it on meeting customer needs, where it belongs."[15] The fundamental shift for businesses in the 1990s is from managing departments to managing processes.

People in different functional departments hate each other.

Why don't companies already manage their processes? Usually they don't manage their processes because processes are largely invisible, and no one has overall responsibility for process performance. In most companies, I have found that virtually no one understands an entire process. Very few people even understand the portion of the

The reason companies don't manage processes is because they are largely invisible.

process that exists in their department. The scariest part is that the group with the single weakest understanding of what is really happening in the company is management. Even management just one level away from the work has little understanding — not to mention the executives many layers of bureaucracy away from the real work. When confronted with the labyrinthine map of their company's processes, the response from executives is invariably one of shock, then disbelief. Few actions will spur an executive to action faster than confronting him or her with a process map for a supposedly simple process (like fulfilling an order) that *covers an entire wall.*

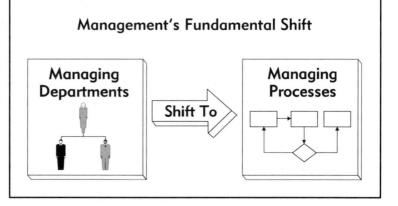

Figure 4.6

To get horizontal, companies must shift from managing departments to managing processes.

Companies that organize around processes sometimes find unexpected benefits. The CEO of Thermos Corporation galvanized his company by replacing the functional organization with flexible interdisciplinary teams, and to his delight, "innovation blossomed and new product development took off." The result — a thermo-electric grill that has red-hot sales. Thermos predicts that the cooker could boost the market share for electric grills from 2% to 20% over the next few years.[16]

"Getting horizontal" is not easy. Untangling years of bureaucracy to uncover the underlying processes is a time consuming and painstaking exercise. For instance, AT&T's Network Services division identified around 130 processes before narrowing them down to 13 core ones.[17] As difficult as it will seem, documenting processes must be done — companies that wait will simply find themselves that much further behind the competition.

Total Process Management emphasizes identifying and documenting business processes as the first step toward becoming a "horizontal company." I believe that every process should be documented and fully understood by everyone participating in the process. Only then can every employee achieve the understanding necessary to make effective business decisions — a prerequisite for any real form of empowerment. Part 3 of the methodology, "Evaluate the Current Environment," covers process mapping in detail.

Systems

Information technology is one of the key enablers for performance improvement. The development and capacity of information technology are expanding exponentially. The potential for leveraging technology for competitive advantage is unlike any other time in history. Obviously, Total Process Management emphasizes information technology as an important tool for performance improvement. Although

Information technology is one of the key enablers for performance improvement.

the range of technologies is virtually endless, below are a few of the more common technologies being employed today for performance improvement.

Distributed client/server computing. This is not about reducing corporate costs for maintaining a mainframe computer infrastructure as many people claim. Some studies say client/server is no less expensive once you factor in transition costs and the growing cost of "middle-ware" that ties all the technologies together.[18] Rather, the real advantage of client/server architectures is *flexibility* — the ability to respond quickly to meet changing markets and competitive conditions.

Electronic Data Interchange (EDI). EDI has been used at companies such as Wal-Mart to "become borderless" and tie in suppliers electronically. As Wal-Mart's stock price performance shows, they have reaped the benefits of EDI in speed, efficiency, and customer responsiveness.

Image Processing. Could the paperless corporation really be about to happen? For a long time, it has been on the horizon, but it has never arrived. The time might now be at hand. With powerful image scanning technology and workflow software, many companies are dumping paper and going electronic.

Expert systems. Companies everywhere have a few priceless experts who know all there is to know and can solve anything. Imagine being able to shrink them and put them into a computer so that everyone could access the information and be as smart as that one expert. That is what expert systems do. Companies from insurance agencies to software manufacturers are leveraging its capability to enhance productivity and quality.

Groupware. This software provides an on-line environment where organizational learning can progress at an unparalleled rate. Groupware lets widely dispersed employees communicate on topics such as new product development as if they were in the same room.

Other Technologies. The list of technologies could go on and on, but a few others deserve at least honorable mention. Other technologies to explore are hand-held devices, multimedia, cellular telecommunications, wide-area and local-area networks (WAN/LAN), executive information systems (EIS), and bar code printing and scanning.

Structure

Structure relates to both the physical layout of the work environment and the organizational hierarchy. A poorly conceived or unplanned physical work environment layout can be a significant barrier to productivity. Substantial performance improvements in speed, accuracy, and efficiency will usually result from better workplace design. I have seen departments in *separate buildings* that routinely needed to interact to conduct business — imagine the time wasted by people going back and forth! In addition, organizing around process usually results in some changes to the physical work layout.

Organization hierarchy reveals excessive levels of management and managerial spans of control that are too narrow. Targeting these areas for improvement can result in large returns in productivity and organizational efficiency. Total Process Management addresses both the physical layout and organizational hierarchy dimensions of structure in providing an overall solution for performance improvement.

Structure relates to both the physical layout of the work environment as well as the organizational hierarchy.

People

People includes culture, performance measures and rewards, and employee skills. *People* is the broadest of the organizational levers for change, the hardest to pin down, and the most important for obtaining lasting performance improvement.

Culture is defined by corporate values and self-image. If you want to find out what a company's culture is, just start doing things out of the ordinary — you will find out quickly when you begin to break the unspoken corporate rules (values). Corporate values include respect for the individual, service, risk taking, formal/informal chains of command, rule following/breaking, and internal competitiveness versus cooperation.

> *People is the broadest of the organizational levers for change, the hardest to pin down, and the most important for obtaining lasting performance improvement.*

Values must evolve with changing environmental conditions, or they can contribute to corporate decline. IBM found this out — one of their values was employment for life. What were they to do when they found themselves hopelessly overstaffed and needing to reduce costs? Letting people go would violate their cultural value and cause untold harm to employee trust and morale — which is what eventually happened. Another example is entrepreneurial start-ups. As they mature, they must give up the everyone-for-themselves value for teamwork and cooperation. This is a difficult transition at best.

There isn't a single set of cultural values that are the right values to have. However, each company must look at their values and see if the behavior that they want of their employees is supported. Certain values do characterize world-class companies. These values include customer obsession, quality, speed, profitability, teamwork, innovation, risk-taking, efficiency, external focus, continuous improvement, and corporate learning.

A second component of culture is a company's self-image, which creates "filters" through which information must pass. Information available for decision making that is inconsistent with the self-image is eliminated or changed. For years IBM ignored Compaq as insignificant. Compaq ignored Dell, and Dell ignored Gateway 2000. Each company in turn gained market share through the blind spots in the other company's self-image. The CEO of Ameritech, William Weiss, determined that his company's self-image needed overhauling because, "If our culture just kept plugging along, competitors would just devour our markets. . . . Our culture had no instinct for competition. We had an entitlement philosophy, believing that we were a monopoly because it was right to be a monopoly." He continued, "Finally I decided to drop a bomb. I had to intervene on a massive basis."[19]

Self-image can also cause companies to miss emerging market opportunities. Consider the fact that K-Mart was once the king of discount retailing and how Wal-Mart has come virtually out of nowhere to dominate that marketplace. Despite evidence of Wal-Mart's success using innovative techniques, K-Mart clung to the "classic textbook approach that accounted for its original success."[20]

For process improvement, culture can be a formidable foe. "People and culture — the human systems of a company — are what make or break any change initiative."[21] A recent survey of over 500 companies that had restructured their operations found that the top barriers to change were culturally related.[22] I have seen hardened CEOs stymied by organizational stonewalling caused by cultural barriers to change. What good is it to streamline a process to reduce cycle time in organizations that do not value speed? Without cultural support for changes, they will fail miserably. Total Process Management provides tools for understanding the explicit and implicit cultural values and techniques for cultural change.

Another component of *people* is performance measurement and rewards. The old adage that you can't improve what you don't measure is still true. Although some companies measure non-financial performance, almost none measure *process* performance. Besides measurement, companies must pay attention to performance rewards. People will do what you reward, not what you say. In my experience, companies rarely reward the performance that they really want to encourage. Total Process Management includes review and modification of performance measures and rewards as a key element of overall process improvement.

People and culture — the human systems of a company — are what make or break any change initiative.[21]

Finally, people must have the skills to operate effectively in this changing world. Both PVI and PVR require new skills of employees. People comfortable with a command and control management style cannot transition to an empowered, process-oriented style without significant retraining. Corporate training and education systems, requirements for employee retooling, must be established or enhanced to accommodate Total Process Management.

A RECIPE FOR 5
SUCCESS

The Total Process Management Methodology

*"Thus times do shift, each thing his
turn does hold; new things succeed, as
former things grow old."*
— *Robert Herrick*

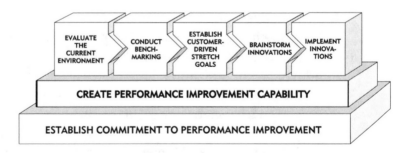

There are seven parts to the Total Process Management (TPM) methodology. The first two parts form the foundation for performance improvement. The remaining five parts of the methodology form the process improvement cycle. In this chapter, I provide an overview of each part. TPM, like any methodology, is only effective if executed properly. The final part of this chapter provides some tips for succeeding at Total Process Management.

Any tool or methodology should be interpreted and applied appropriately given individual corporate circumstances and needs. Flexibility is one of the key messages regarding Total Process Management. The director of product development at Herman Miller advises, "Don't negate the uniqueness of your company by adopting an off-the-shelf quality program."[1] TPM is no exception. Airline pilots say, "Any landing you can walk away from is a good one." Something similar can be said for performance improvement — any performance improvement is better than none "even if it ain't pretty."

Any tool or methodology should be interpreted and applied only as appropriate.

Obviously, I advocate implementing the full methodology. Your company gives up potential performance improvement when the implementation is incomplete. However, quickly achieving some results is better than following a methodology step-by-step until it's too late for the improvements to help you. A cautionary word — organizational resistance is not a valid excuse for incomplete implementation of the methodology. That is just an excuse for failure in executive will.

The Total Process Management methodology is composed of two sections. The first section is called the foundation section and consists of Part 1, Establish Commitment to Performance Improvement, and Part 2, Create Performance Improvement Capability.

The second section, the process improvement cycle, consists of the remaining five parts of the methodology.

Implementing the foundation section broadly across the company creates a process improvement culture. In this environment, organizational sub-units throughout the company execute the process improvement cycle continuously. The cycle is: selecting the process to improve, understanding the process, benchmarking, setting customer-driven stretch targets, brainstorming innovations, and following through with implementation of the innovations. Despite the obvious benefits of this approach, it has one significant drawback — it takes a long time to do.

Another approach provides for just-in-time performance improvement. This is most commonly employed for process value reinvention, but it also has some application for process improvement. In this approach, the foundation section is applied only for the process targeted for improvement instead of for the whole company. Executive support, training, and the improvement cycle are applied to a limited number of people and for a limited scope. For process reinvention, just-in-time performance improvement is applied to the project team. For process value improvement, individual workgroups can justify a project and obtain the necessary training and executive support. This approach is effective for companies needing quick action.

How do we cultivate the motivation to change?

Part 1. Establish Commitment to Performance Improvement. This part of TPM addresses the will to change — the top-down communication and enforcement of the need to change. It involves defining the market forces that are driving the need to change; refining mission, strategy, and culture; communicating with the organization; removing barriers to change; and rewarding performance.

How do we obtain the skills needed to implement change?

Part 2. Create Performance Improvement Capability. This part of TPM involves training on the skills required for performance improvement and for organizing around processes. It includes the performance improvement principles, problem analysis tools and techniques, and creative brainstorming.

What are we doing today?

Part 3. Evaluate the Current Environment. Before you can hope to improve your processes, you must understand them. This part of TPM documents and evaluates each of the four organizational levers for change: process, systems, structure, and people. Here we document and evaluate the current environment through people involved in executing the process, as well as customers and suppliers to the process.

What are other companies doing?

Part 4. Conduct Benchmarking. Benchmarking gives a view of the performance levels achieved by our competitors and by world-class companies. It is a source of ideas for improving our own processes. The information from benchmarking helps set stretch goals and feeds innovations in creative brainstorming.

How much improvement do customers want?

Part 5. Establish Customer-Driven Stretch Goals. In this part of TPM, we meet with customers of the process, both internal and external, and determine their requirements for the process in the dimensions of speed, cost, and quality. This information, coupled with the results of benchmarking, is used to develop customer-driven stretch performance goals for use in creative brainstorming.

What ideas do we have about how to improve performance?

Part 6. Brainstorm Innovations. In this part we seek to reinvent our processes through paradise visioning.[2] This involves a series of creative brainstorming sessions followed by increasingly analytical "focus group" sessions. "Change actions" are the results from these sessions. Change actions document what will be done, by whom, when it will be done, and why we're doing it. This will drive the implementation of improvements in the final part of the methodology.

How will we turn ideas into results?

Part 7. Implement Innovations. This is where results begin to be realized. This part of TPM addresses the activities required to implement the change actions generated during creative brainstorming. It discusses practical methods for testing and rolling out innovations, and for tracking them to completion to ensure that expected results are achieved.

KEYS TO SUCCESS IN TOTAL PROCESS MANAGEMENT

- ❖ Sponsor change at the top
- ❖ Address all four organizational levers for change
- ❖ Establish Total Process Management capability
- ❖ Focus on the right processes
- ❖ Set goals and deliver results
- ❖ Cultivate organizational support

The Total Process Management methodology, by itself, is no guarantee of success in achieving meaningful performance improvement results. After all, approximately 70% of process improvement efforts fail.[3] The purpose of this portion of the chapter is to point out some of the most common pitfalls and how you can avoid them. Follow these keys to success and your company will increase substantially the likelihood of staying out of that 70%!

Sponsor Change at the Top

Organizational change is always difficult. Process value reinvention is particularly difficult because it involves dramatic, sudden change. It will be resisted at every level of the organization by employees entrenched in the current business methods or who are defending organizational turf. Therefore, the change effort must be supported at the highest level of executive management possible (preferably at the President or Chief Executive

One of the greatest pains to human nature is the pain of a new idea.

— Walter Bagehot

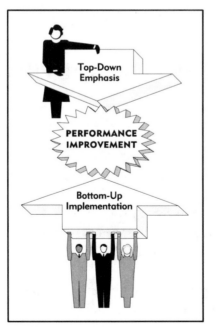

Figure 5.1

What role has management involvement played in the success or failure of change initiatives in your company?

Officer level), or it will be difficult to achieve meaningful results. Total Process Management involves top-down emphasis and bottom-up implementation.

Address All Four Organizational Levers for Change

Companies are complex systems that behave like living organisms. Processes are woven into the very fabric of these organisms. Performance improvement requires the painstaking exercise of coaxing apart all the interwoven dependencies. In the end, you must address all four organizational levers for change for TPM to be successful.

Process. This involves the flow of tasks and activities that collectively deliver value to a customer.

Systems. Information technology is a key enabler for performance improvement.

Structure. This relates to both the physical layout of the work environment as well as the organizational hierarchy. Targeting these areas for improvement can result in large returns in productivity and organizational efficiency.

People. The People dimension includes the elements of culture, company values, and individual skills. This dimension is important for achieving organizational acceptance of change.

Establish Total Process Management Capability

The devil is in the details! As with anything else, competent execution is essential to the success of Total Process Management. Companies cannot expect to improve performance effectively without adequate expertise or tools.

Expertise. There are three mechanisms for obtaining process improvement expertise:

- ❖ Hire experienced personnel
- ❖ Obtain specialized training
- ❖ Purchase qualified consulting services

Hire Experienced Personnel. There is nothing that replaces the skill and knowledge that comes from having done something before. Training is not enough — use consultants or hire someone with previous TPM experience.

Companies cannot expect to improve performance effectively without adequate expertise or tools.

Obtain Specialized Training. TPM has a distinct methodology. It is essential that everyone involved in TPM be trained on the principles and techniques.

Purchase Qualified Consulting Services. If your company is short on TPM experience or on available personnel, consider using qualified consultants. The key word is "qualified." Be certain that the consultants have a proven track record for success and provide staff experienced in Total Process Management.

Tools. Total Process Management has three fundamental tools.

- ❖ Process mapping software
- ❖ Project management software
- ❖ Statistical analysis and problem-solving tools

Process Mapping Software. Process maps are used in every aspect of Total Process Management. As a result, powerful, flexible process mapping tools are the life blood of TPM practitioners.

Project Management Software. Process value reinvention projects are massive affairs. They are every bit as complex as many system development projects. Few information systems professionals would dream of tackling a new system without project management software. The same should be true of the process reinvention team. Each project (and sub-project if needed) should be planned and tracked to completion using powerful project management software. The added effort in establishing and tracking a project plan will more than pay for itself in the smooth execution of the project.

Statistical Analysis and Problem-Solving Tools. Process improvement relies heavily on tools such as scatter diagrams, Pareto charts, and run charts. These are used in creative brainstorming, problem solving, and tracking process performance. Automated tools can dramatically reduce the effort required to develop these analyses.

Focus on the Right Processes

It is no fun to climb the process improvement ladder only to find that it is propped against the wrong wall. It is essential to pick the right processes for your projects. Usually, these are broken processes that are strategically important and feasible to repair.

- ❖ Broken processes
- ❖ Strategically important
- ❖ Feasible to achieve results

Broken Processes. The key qualification for gaining organizational support is a common awareness by the employees that the process is broken. Employees know that a process is dysfunctional sooner than management because they are closer to the processes. Employees need a reason to change. Why else would they go through all that effort and anguish? Employees need to be able to see that tangible improvements result from the change.

Strategically Important. Total Process Management is conducted at every level. The big benefits (and the big pain) accrue when process value reinvention (PVR) projects are conducted for top-level processes. For PVR projects, it is important to pick processes that make a substantial difference on business unit performance. The organizational commitment for this kind of effort has to be based on the knowledge that the company will perform and compete visibly better after the change effort.

Feasible to Achieve Results. Delivering results is what makes people support a change management program. What good is talk about the wonders of TPM if it takes three years to see any results? Apply the "one-year rule" for large TPM projects—only tackle projects that can be completed within one year or break the projects into pieces that can be completed in that time. A diagram of this rule is shown in Figure 5.2.

> *Well done is quickly done.*
> *— Augustus Caesar*

Figure 5.2

How many successful projects can you cite that lasted for over one year?

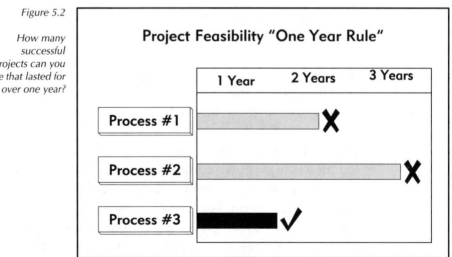

Set Goals and Deliver Results

Many companies lose sight of the ultimate goal in performance improvement — bottom-line results. The CEO of Analog Devices, Ray Stata, kicked off his company's TQM effort with the exhortation: "Quality is free. Go do it." — nothing happened.[4] He learned a key lesson about getting results — tangible performance improvement requires setting stretch goals and measuring to see if actual results are achieved. Too many times the thinking is if you train enough people and preach about benchmarking and assessing customer expectations, then the results will magically appear. They don't.

> The philosophers have only interpreted the world in various ways. The point, however, is to change it.
>
> — Karl Marx

Cultivate Organizational Support

In desperation to find the magic pill that will cure their competitive ills, many companies have overwhelmed their employees with great ideas that weren't. The common refrain from employees is, "Here comes another MBMA (Management By Magazine Article) brainstorm from our leaders." What will make these tired, skeptical, and cynical employees think Total Process Management is any different from other improvement fads? Three actions will help build acceptance of TPM.

- ❖ Establish credibility
- ❖ Create quick wins
- ❖ Communicate early and often

Establish Credibility. The organization wants to know that the people implementing change have listened and understand their work. These are strong reasons for developing accurate and detailed process maps. Also, selecting respected employees as change champions will build employee confidence that their interests are represented.

Quick Wins. Organizational enthusiasm can be built and maintained by delivering some results in a shorter time. Identify opportunities for improvement as early as the first interviews. Implement these ideas immediately and turn them into quick wins. Herald your victories to the organization.

Communication. The quickest way to generate fear in an organization is to keep secrets. Since nothing can be kept secret anyway, employees immediately assume that bad news is pending. The cure for this is simple. Communicate! Tell the organization what you are planning to do. Tell them why. Tell them what progress is being made. Trumpet quick wins. Involve them on teams. Ask their opinions. Make TPM a topic at company and departmental meetings. Communicate your message "seven times and in seven different ways."

TOTAL
PROCESS
MANAGEMENT
FOUNDATION

CREATE PERFORMANCE IMPROVEMENT CAPABILITY

ESTABLISH COMMITMENT TO PERFORMANCE IMPROVEMENT

TPM Part 1

Establish Commitment to Performance Improvement

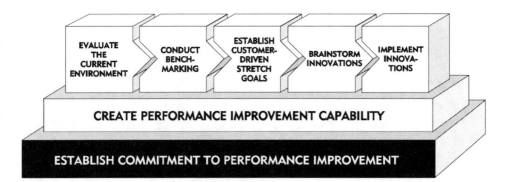

SAILING A STORMY SEA 6

Creating Organizational Will to Change

Anyone can hold the helm when the sea is calm.

—Publilius Syrus

People resist change. Total Process Management asks that people rethink their institutionalized ways of working, and try entirely new ways. Overcoming the resistance to change requires unwavering executive commitment. In addition, it requires from management a deliberate and persistent effort to develop organizational support for new ways of doing business.

There is nothing more difficult to take in hand, more perilous to conduct, or more uncertain in its success, than to take the lead in the introduction of a new order of things.
— Niccolò Machiavelli, 1532

This chapter answers the question, *How do we cultivate the motivation to change?* The topics in this chapter include

- Adapt the TPM Foundation
- Secure Executive Commitment to Total Process Management
- Establish Total Process Management Infrastructure
- Identify Change Drivers
- Refine Corporate Mission and Strategy
- Identify and Refine Cultural Values
- Establish Communication Plan
- Cultivate Organizational Support
- Remove Barriers to Process Improvement
- Measure Performance and Reward Results

ADAPT THE TPM FOUNDATION

The first two parts of the methodology form the foundation section. These two parts establish the organizational will to change and the skill to change, respectively. The foundation portion of TPM is essential for sustaining long-term performance improvement. TPM can be executed without establishing the foundation, but any potential performance improvements are going to be very difficult to implement in the face of organizational resistance, and unlikely to last once they are implemented.

There is a method for adapting Total Process Management so that it can be implemented for quick benefits without fully implementing the foundation section. This approach provides for just-in-time performance improvement. In

this technique, the foundation section is applied only for the processes targeted for improvement. This is particularly effective in process reinvention where only the workgroups participating in the process can be selected to establish the commitment and skills required to implement TPM performance improvements.

The just-in-time approach can also be used in process improvement, but will be less effective. The way for it to be effective is to identify workgroups that are motivated to change, have specific objectives for performance improvement, and provide them with training and executive support for TPM. Their successes can lead the way for acceptance of TPM on a broader organizational level.

SECURE EXECUTIVE COMMITMENT TO TOTAL PROCESS MANAGEMENT

Change can be successful without executive commitment and support, but only on a very small scale. Sponsorship high in the organization leads to a broader and deeper impact on performance improvement. Why is that the case? Processes cut across organizational boundaries. To improve overall performance, processes must be considered in total. Improving just the portion of the process that exists in a workgroup could reduce the overall process performance.

It is a rough road that leads to the heights of greatness.
— Seneca

Because processes cut across departments, change requires a sponsor who transcends the authority of any single department head. Change cannot be led from low in an organization, because it will be blocked by organizational boundaries like "waves dashing against a seawall."[1] The sponsor must be an executive who is accountable for all the affected departments. As you might guess, this person is ordinarily the business unit head or CEO. Michael Hammer says that the person sponsoring the change must have a lot of clout, "Because many people are going to need to be clouted."[2] The following example illustrates this point. The leadership at one company where the process redesign effort was unsuccessful was described as having "the nominal sponsorship of someone two layers down in the organization, but in actuality, it was driven by someone four layers down. The ultimate redesign focused on narrow contract and back office sales processes and never really went anywhere in terms of implementation."[3]

Ultimately, the executive sponsor will be required at some point in the change process to play the heavy, and enforce the change effort. For instance, one CEO who replaced over half of the key positions in his company said, "We have 128 key positions in this company; we've changed the people in 69 of them."[4] In order to succeed, an executive has to be "a visionary, a motivator, and a leg breaker."[5] At Aetna, one of the ten lessons CEO Ronald E. Compton learned from their change effort is that the weak link is executive will.[6] Without it, the organization will "stare you down" and the improvement effort will fail.

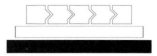

The CEO of an $11 billion company believes that few people will accept voluntarily some of the changes required for real performance improvement.

> *The best way I know to get people to accept the need to change is to not give them a choice. The organization has to know that there is a leader at the top who has made up his mind, that he is surrounded by leaders who have made up their minds, and that they are going to drive forward no matter what.*[7]

One key to success is for executives to dedicate their time to the change effort, particularly early in the process. What kind of time commitment? Maybe 10 to 15 percent? Guess again. How about 20 to 50 percent![8] Authors of a study of more than 100 companies conducting change projects concluded that the most important factor in successful redesign projects was that the executives invested their own time in the project.[9]

The chief way in which executives commit their time is communicating with the organization at all levels about the need to change and about progress being made in the change process. Another way that executives can invest their time is to take training in the methodology along with the other employees. Executives can also spend time in managing progress of the change effort, allocating resources, removing barriers to improvement, celebrating successes, and enforcing the change directive.

It is vitally important for executives who are spearheading the change effort to be positive role models for the organization, to "walk the talk." The CEO at Rubbermaid,

Wolfgang Schmidt, required training of all of his employees in the new change management approach. To "walk the talk," he took over 60 hours of training with the other employees. He said that he ". . . had to be visibly part of it. People look to see if you just talk about it or actually do it."[10]

Every expectation of the general corporate population should apply doubly to the executive team. If the executives are preaching empowerment, they should think twice before overriding a decision made at lower levels. If executives are asking for financial sacrifices, they should start by making twice as much sacrifice. The key point is for executives to set an example for their employees. In the end, employees will do what you do, not what you say.

ESTABLISH TOTAL PROCESS MANAGEMENT INFRASTRUCTURE

The best way to implement a change management approach such as Total Process Management is to establish a formal infrastructure to support the effort. The key roles and their relationships are shown in Figure 6.1.

As stated earlier in this chapter, the executive sponsor is the person ultimately responsible for ensuring that Total Process Management is successful in its process improvement and process reinvention versions. Key responsibilities of the executive sponsor include the following:

Figure 6.1

What is the
infrastructure
for managing
change in your
company?

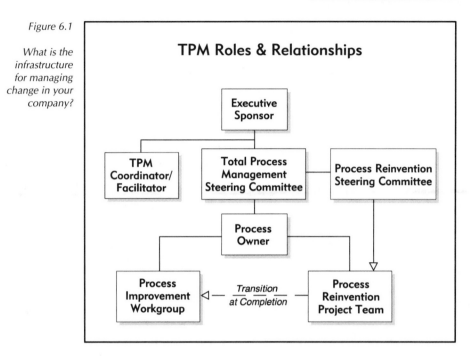

TPM Roles & Relationships

Executive
Sponsor

TPM
Coordinator/
Facilitator

Total Process
Management
Steering Committee

Process Reinvention
Steering Committee

Process
Owner

Process
Improvement
Workgroup

*Transition
at Completion*

Process
Reinvention
Project Team

- ❖ Provide the "executive will" required to overcome organizational resistance to change.
- ❖ Serve as the "chief communicator" of the need to change and of improvement successes.
- ❖ Obtain the necessary resources and remove barriers to improvement.
- ❖ Establish the Total Process Management steering committee.
- ❖ Establish and staff the TPM Coordinator/Facilitator role.
- ❖ Assign the process owners and establish the process owners' authority over the processes.

There are usually two steering committees for Total Process Management; however, one can be a subset of the other. The first is the *Total Process Management steering committee*. Since TPM ultimately involves everyone in the company, this committee should be staffed by senior executives from across the entire business unit. The TPM steering committee is responsible for initiating process value improvement throughout the organization, and for establishing the *Process Reinvention Steering Committee(s)*. The TPM steering committee is accountable to the executive sponsor for overall organizational acceptance of Total Process Management and for achieving tangible performance improvements through TPM. It is common practice in companies successful in implementing change to base a significant portion of executive pay on success of the change effort.[11]

The TPM steering committee has the critical role of coordinating and aligning the various PVI and PVR activities. Most companies will roll out process value improvement and conduct multiple process reinvention projects at the same time. To achieve the desired results and minimize conflict and confusion, it is essential that the goals and scope of these efforts be aligned and their activities coordinated. Besides authorizing projects and activities, the committee must also *kill* the projects that no longer have a purpose or have been superseded. This may seem like a trivial point, but not when you consider how many projects end up in limbo and die a slow withering death. Even these neglected projects consume resources — better to eliminate them altogether and focus the organization on the projects you really want to achieve.

The *process reinvention steering committee* can be the same as the TPM steering committee, or more commonly, a subset

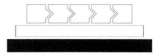

of it. Process reinvention projects are focused on a single process and affect a limited portion of the organization. Executives from the organizational elements impacted by the project should be selected for this steering committee. Since an organization may have multiple PVR projects going simultaneously, a company may need to have several different PVR steering committees. In this case, each of the steering committees could be expected to have different members. The process value reinvention steering committees are accountable to the TPM steering committee and to the executive sponsor for the success of their respective projects.

Both types of steering committees have accountability for performance improvement *results*. Results start with establishing a clear mission for Total Process Management and goals for expected performance improvement. The steering committees have responsibility for monitoring progress of the process improvement and reinvention efforts, and for allocating resources and removing obstacles required for achieving the improvement goals. Also, the steering committees evaluate and establish the priority of process reinvention projects.

The *TPM facilitator/coordinator* should be a full time position and may require additional staff depending on the size of the organization. This role already exists in many companies under titles such as VP of Quality or Manager of Process Reengineering. This position should report directly to the executive sponsor to have the "political immunity" required for any degree of objectivity. Following are the responsibilities for this position.

- ❖ Serve as the organization's expert in the Total Process Management methodology.
- ❖ Provide technical advice to the steering committees and the process owners as needed.
- ❖ Train the organization in the TPM methodology.
- ❖ Assist in obtaining internal staffing and consulting resources for process value reinvention projects.
- ❖ Assist in conducting the PVR projects including project management, interviewing and process mapping, benchmarking, setting stretch targets, visioning, and change planning.
- ❖ Monitor change action implementation and report to the executive sponsor and steering committees as appropriate.
- ❖ Serve as facilitator for process value improvement brainstorming and problem-solving sessions.

The *process owner* has a key role in the organization. Business processes cut across organizational boundaries to deliver value to the customer. One of the main contributors to inefficient processes is the hand-offs where processes cross departmental lines. To optimize a process, companies must evaluate change across the entire process, disregarding individual departments. This requires a process owner.

In order to optimize a process, companies must evaluate change across the entire process, disregarding individual departments.

The executive sponsor and TPM steering committee must identify the process owner, and empower that person with authority to implement change across multiple departments. Usually, this person works in the department with the most to gain or lose from the effectiveness of the pro-

cess. For instance, an order fulfillment process typically involves the sales, manufacturing, warehousing/shipping, and accounting departments. Someone in the sales organization will most likely be selected as the process owner. The sales department has contact with and responsibility to the customer that drives the activities in the other departments.

The process owner's responsibility is to ensure that the total process is both effective and efficient, and that performance is continually improved. Other responsibilities include the following:

- ❖ Ensure that detailed process maps are developed and maintained.
- ❖ Ensure that the *process members* (everyone involved in the process) understand the *entire* process, and how their jobs affect the rest of the process.
- ❖ Coordinate training in Total Process Management for process members.
- ❖ Establish process value improvement objectives, convene PVI workgroups, and ensure that process members work together to achieve the objectives.
- ❖ Participate in nominating and selecting candidates for process value reinvention projects.
- ❖ Ensure that the objectives of PVR projects are met and that the associated change actions are implemented.
- ❖ Report to the steering committees on results achieved both through PVI and PVR.

Process value improvement workgroups are temporary teams composed of selected process members who come together to meet specific performance improvement objectives. Once the objectives are met, the workgroup usually dissolves. PVI workgroups can be convened by the process owner to tackle specific improvement objectives. Process members can also originate PVI workgroups to address their own performance improvement or problem-solving objectives. The PVI workgroups follow the same five-part Process Improvement Cycle in the TPM methodology used by the process value reinvention teams, but on a much smaller scale. PVI workgroups may involve third parties from uninvolved departments, customers, consultants, and others to achieve increased objectivity in brainstorming innovations. Results from the PVI effort (both good and bad) should be included in the team member's overall performance evaluation.

Figure 6.2

Effective process reinvention requires participation from objective third parties, technical advisers, and process members.

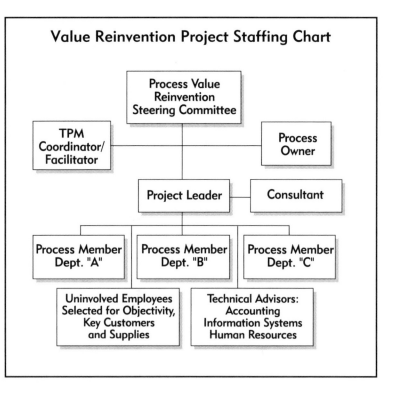

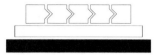

Process value reinvention teams are responsible for conducting the PVR projects and achieving the performance improvement objectives. The teams, which should be limited to 5 to 15 people to maintain the team's effectiveness, consist of selected process members along with representatives from other departments and possibly one or more consultants. The chart in Figure 6.2 shows typical PVR project team staffing.

The PVR teams should be assigned full time to the project and be composed of the company's best employees. It is a tall order to ask managers to give up their best people when they have performance objectives of their own to meet. However, it is essential if the project is to achieve significant long-term performance improvement results. After all, you are asking these people to *reinvent* key business processes for your company — do you really want to put this responsibility in the hands of average or below-average performers? One company learned this lesson the hard way. A mediocre sales manager was assigned to head an improvement project because his contribution wouldn't be missed in the field. Because this manager lacked the credibility and skills to lead, the project ultimately failed.[12]

Besides process members from each affected department participating on the team, every project should include technical advisors from key groups. The technical advisors can participate in any part of the project, but are particularly effective during paradise visioning and focus group sessions in Part 6, Brainstorm Innovations, of the TPM methodology.

- ❖ Uninvolved employees from other areas in the company can provide an element of objectivity and new ideas to the improvement effort.
- ❖ Information systems employees should be represented to help in identifying key enabling technologies.
- ❖ Personnel expertise is essential in evaluating and developing the "structure" and "people" organizational levers for change.
- ❖ Internal customers and suppliers make excellent contributors.
- ❖ External customers and suppliers should be added to the team when the integrity of confidential corporate information is not an issue. These people can bring eye-opening reality to misconceptions about problems and requirements.

How do you get the people who invented the processes and participate in them every day to think outside them? This may require the use of outside consultants. Qualified consultants can relate experiences from other companies, share best practices, and provide the important element of objectivity. The reengineering manager for one company advises using consultants for their subject matter expertise. She reportedly has used over a dozen different consulting firms. She selects the best one each time for the particular process being reengineered.

How do you get the people who invented the processes and participate in them every day to think outside of them?

When the process value reinvention project gets to Part 7, Implement Innovations, of the TPM methodology, the innovations, recorded as change actions, begin to be implemented. At this point, the process owner involves the pro-

cess members in implementation of the improvements. Ultimately, the PVR innovations will be fully implemented, and responsibility for on-going improvement will transition to the process value improvement workgroups. This is a key point — this transition provides the sustaining action required for PVR changes to be successful in the long term.

IDENTIFY CHANGE DRIVERS

Change drivers, as the name implies, are those internal and external business conditions that are "driving" the need to change. It is best to identify and document the change drivers before implementing Total Process Management. However, many change drivers surface from benchmarking and other portions of the process improvement cycle. This information is used in communications with the organization to build credibility and organizational consensus for the need to change.

You have to give people a reason to do something differently.[13]
— Lawrence Bossidy

John F. Welch, CEO of General Electric, makes the following point about change drivers:

How do you bring people into the change process? Start with reality. Get all the facts out. Give people the rationale for change, laying it out in the clearest, most dramatic terms. When everybody gets the same facts, they'll generally come to the same conclusion. Only after everyone agrees on the reality, and resistance is lowered, can you begin to get buy-in to the needed change.[14]

AlliedSignal's CEO, Lawrence Bossidy says, "To inaugurate large scale change, you may have to create the burning platform. You have to give people a reason to do things differently. Scaring people isn't the answer. You try to appeal to them. The more they understand why you want to change, the easier it is to commit to it."[15] At General Electric, the following change drivers were identified.

❖ The increasing global character of markets and competition
❖ Slow top-line growth of the business
❖ Emerging growth opportunities
❖ The need to be a nimble organization
❖ The competition's improved product development cycle times and overall responsiveness to customers[16]

Most companies are virtually fighting for their lives against fierce competition, and are in dire need of overhauling their business processes. In these circumstances, it is relatively easy to prove the need for change. However, if your organization is one of the lucky few that has everything going its way, senior management may want to "start a fire" to avoid the complacency that leads to diminishing competitive performance. Jack Welch advises, "Success often breeds self-confidence and arrogance along with reluctance to change. The bureaucracy builds up. The people start to believe they're invulnerable. Before they know it, the world changes and they've got to react."[17] Don't let this happen to you. As Michael Walsh, CEO of Tenneco says, "There are two kinds of businesses in the United States: those that are heading for the cliff and know it, and those that are heading the same way but don't know it."[18]

REFINE CORPORATE MISSION AND STRATEGY

Mission and strategy form the top of the Total Process Management constellation. Mission defines the purpose of the organization — strategy defines how you are going to achieve it. Mission and strategy form the context for employees to make decisions to further the corporate objective. Without them, performance improvement is impossible, with or without a change management methodology. Does this sound obvious? Surprisingly few companies have an effective mission and strategy that are communicated and fully understood throughout the company. When conducting process value reinvention interviews, I frequently ask, "Do you know what the corporate mission and strategy is, and how it relates to what you do?" Most people do not know the answer. Even when they are told the mission and strategy, they have *no idea of what it means to their work.*

Very few employees can relate the corporate mission to the work that they do.

If mission and strategy are missing or poorly understood, different departments will be working at cross-purposes. This is the equivalent of hitching powerful horses to each side of a wagon so that they are all pulling in different directions. The horses can pull until they drop from exhaustion and that wagon still isn't going to move. Many companies drive their employees to do more when the problem isn't lack of effort — the problem is everyone pulling in different directions.

Before implementing Total Process Management, executives must make sure they clearly understand and can articulate the corporate mission and strategy. Take the time to rethink mission and strategy. Union Carbide took the time to change their focus and shifted from specialty products to commodity chemicals. This rethinking drove Union Carbide's intention for their reengineering efforts, "to seek its competitive advantage in the lowest possible manufacturing costs and provide added value in delivery and service."[19]

Mission statements are relatively constant. Although they should change, they should do so slowly through an evolutionary process. Strategies should be relatively volatile. They should change as frequently as environmental conditions require. A good mission statement is brief, to the point, not too detailed, captures the essential purpose of the organization, and is easily understood and remembered.

IDENTIFY AND REFINE CULTURAL VALUES

Cultural values are profound influences on employee behavior and decision making. The two kinds of cultural values are explicit and implicit. Explicit values are docu-

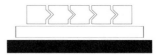

mented, actively communicated, and understood throughout the organization. Implicit values are just as powerful
but are not obvious, talked about, or intentional. A certain amount of researching and interviewing employees
is usually required to surface implicit values. Implicit values can be very destructive to the change effort. Because
the change leaders do not know they are there, they don't
understand why change efforts aren't succeeding. Like
giant underwater rocks, implicit values lurk until an un-
suspecting ship (the change effort) runs up on them. Then
it's too late — the ship is sunk.

In implementing Total Process Management, executives
should evaluate their cultural values and determine if the
behavior the executives want to encourage is supported.
If not, they should initiate action to change the behavior.
For example, U.S. Vice-Presi-
dent Al Gore, in his quest to "reinvent government," must first
overcome powerful cultural
forces. From my experience in
working with government
agencies, their values include risk avoidance, lifetime employment, excessive rules, command and control management styles, and hiring practices that do not always at-
tract employees with the right skill sets. Those are a lot of
submerged rocks waiting for Al's boat to come along.

*Hidden cultural values are like
underwater rocks constantly
threatening to sink your ship.*

Cultural values are embedded over a long time through
behavior modeling by organizational leaders, frequent
and two-way communication, and rewards for people
demonstrating the desired behavior. Companies should
be cautioned to change only a few values at a time. (One
at a time can be a challenge just by itself!) There isn't a

single set of values that are the "right" values to have. However, world-class companies demonstrate one or more of the following values.

- ❖ Customer obsession
- ❖ Quality
- ❖ Speed
- ❖ Profitability and low cost structures
- ❖ Teamwork
- ❖ Empowered workers
- ❖ Innovation
- ❖ Risk-taking
- ❖ Process efficiency
- ❖ External focus
- ❖ Continuous improvement
- ❖ Corporate learning
- ❖ Respect for the individual
- ❖ Community service
- ❖ Honesty and integrity

ESTABLISH COMMUNICATION PLAN

Everything that the management team does or doesn't do sends a message. There is no such thing as a secret project. Just the mere absence of key employees, meeting off-site about the "secret" change effort, will initiate rumors, gossip, and innuendo. The choice is simple — either communicate openly about planned changes or the organization will speculate about them behind management's back in 10,000 private little conversations. Employees' fears are usually worse than the reality of the situation.

An effective communication plan is essential for two reasons: to win employee support and acceptance of organizational change, and to reduce fears so that employees will remain productive while the changes are being implemented. In an extensive study of companies implementing change efforts, one of the top four reasons cited for failure was poor communication.[20] One CEO, new to the position and company, made this comment, "This company is the worst I have ever seen about creating and spreading rumors and innuendo." The reason is that the employees did not have a formal outlet for voicing their questions and fears, so they used informal channels. Inadequate communication invariably leads to "grapevine gossiping" that contributes to a substantial loss in productivity.

So what is it that executives are supposed to communicate? Everything. Executives need to share openly and frankly with employees about everything that is happening and why. Lawrence Bossidy, CEO of AlliedSignal says, "Candor is a way to treat people with dignity. You go out there and answer questions as directly as you can. Sometimes it is difficult, but it earns you credibility."[21] In particular, executives must talk about the change drivers — these provide the *compelling need to change*. They need to talk about cultural values and the behaviors expected from employees. They need to be the primary messenger and bell ringer celebrating the organization's successes in implementing change and improving performance.

How are executives supposed to communicate? They should communicate in every way imaginable. It is critical that executives say their message seven different times in seven different ways, and to every employee. The most effective way to communicate, and the most time-consuming, is any form of face-to-face meeting with small groups of employees. This can include sharing a meal, conducting small group meetings with employees and their managers, scheduling small off-site meetings for pivotal personnel (stakeholders), and participating in town-hall sessions. Other important methods of communication include speeches, memos, PR videos, and use of in-house television broadcasts.

How long are executives supposed to communicate their message? Executives should communicate their message just about forever. Employees must be given a message over and over until they fully understand and internalize it for themselves. When you are talking about change, most employees don't *want* to hear about it, so it will take that much longer to get through to them. Included here is the advice of one consultant writing in the *Harvard Business Review*:

> *It is critical that executives say their message seven different times in seven different ways, and to every employee.*

> *If there is a single rule of communications for leaders, it is this: when you are so sick of talking about something that you can hardly stand it, your message is finally starting to get through. . . . From the point of view of the leaders, who have been working on the change program for months, the message is already stale. But what counts is the point of view of the organization. Have they heard the message? Do they believe it? Do they know what it means? Have they interpreted it for themselves, and have they internalized it? Until managers have listened, watched, and talked*

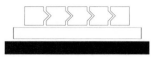

enough to know that the answer to all these questions is yes, they haven't communicated at all.[22]

CULTIVATE ORGANIZATIONAL SUPPORT

If you don't get organizational support, you don't get changes. Period. No amount of cajoling, threats, or fear will get employees to implement your change effort. All these techniques will do is drive the resistance underground. It will show up as unexpected delays, mistakes, false starts, and will ultimately lead to failure. People have to believe in the change effort before they will take part in it. What can leaders do to cultivate organizational support? I recommend these three things: communicate, create quick wins, and build credibility.

> If you don't get organizational support, you don't get changes. Period.

Execute the Communication Plan

I just spent over two pages talking about it. You just spent several weeks developing it. Now execute it. Communicate! People are smarter than you think. They will want to help when they fully understand the need. The following case study shows such a transformation. It was a remarkable experience.

> I was conducting a creative brainstorming session for a process reinvention project. One manager was particularly resistant. I explained several times why the process needed to im-

prove. He saw how the process improvement principles worked to create a more efficient process while improving quality. He viewed the process maps of his area and discussed in detail the redundancies and inefficiencies there. Still he denied the need for changes. Suddenly, something "clicked" for him, and he finally understood. At that moment, he looked at me with this incredible look of surprise. He said, "Then we don't need my entire department!" (He was right, but I hadn't said that specifically.) From that moment on he was the strongest advocate in the room for the process improvement effort.

Gerhard Radtke, Siemens Nixdorf's general manager for service, experienced firsthand the benefits of communicating openly and effectively while leading a change project for corporate headquarters.

Given the potential for resistance, Radtke and his team focused on communicating openly and honestly with the organization as a whole. They told employees how much they would have to reduce headcount and why, emphasizing the facts they had uncovered during the diagnostic phase. "The redesign was not something we were doing because we wanted to do it, we had to do it. We also knew that if we worked with people at all levels to convince them that this could work, we would have their support." Radtke's willingness to keep the lines of communication open was critical to defusing the political resistance that might have developed.[23]

Create Quick Wins

By now, most organizations have been subjected to so many performance improvement approaches that they are reeling under the weight of it all. Companies are full of angry, skeptical, and cynical employees who have been

through it all before. These people have learned how to live through change programs without really changing at all.[24] The only way to reach employees like these is to demonstrate executive commitment to Total Process Management, and to prove, through tangible results, that the new approach really works.

When implementing Total Process Management, leaders should identify several high profile projects that can be completed quickly. These successes can be used to build confidence in the organization that the methodology really works. The results of these quick wins need not necessarily have a high impact on an organization's bottom line, but they do need to have high visibility.

Is your corporate leadership guilty of "Management by Magazine Article"?

> One company I worked with started TPM with a small but visibly broken process to prove the idea. When the project was successful, I was asked to apply TPM to a more mission-critical process. I could almost hear the organization saying "Okay, so it worked once — but will it work again?" The next project was even more successful and the organization finally started to accept that TPM was for real. Almost overnight, I had a dozen managers calling me to be next in line.

Build Credibility

One way in which to build credibility is through candid, two-way communication. People want to know that they have been listened to. Stephen Covey, in *The 7 Habits of Highly Effective People,* calls this "empathic listening." "Empathic listening gets inside another person's frame of reference. You look out through it, you see the world the way they see the world, you understand their paradigm, you understand how they feel."[25]

The essence of his message is that people want to know that you haven't prescribed the medicine before you diagnose the illness. This is absolutely true of the change process. People want to make sure that you understand their business before you go changing it. Some experts advocate jumping straight to "clean slate brainstorming" and skip documenting the current environment. I strongly disagree. Anyone who advocates that approach never tried to get their innovations implemented — because if they had, they would have run head-on into an organization that said, "No way, José. You didn't consider this and this and this."

So, to build credibility, pay your dues and document the current environment. Develop process maps that the organization reviews and agrees are accurate. Include highly competent and respected people on the change teams that have the confidence of the employees. When possible, identify key stakeholders and include them on the project as well. In this way your employees will feel better that their interests will be looked after.

REMOVE BARRIERS TO PROCESS IMPROVEMENT

There are countless barriers to improving process performance. The executive sponsor and the steering commit-

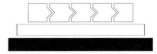

tees are responsible for removing these barriers. The three major barriers to change are lack of resources, lack of sufficient time, and employee fear. The change leaders can deal with the first two fairly easily, but the third is a bit more difficult to tackle.

Insufficient Resources

The change effort requires several different kinds of resources. Top performers are needed to staff the change projects. Access to key people in the organization is necessary to document the current environment. Consulting help may be necessary. The improvement ideas may require the purchase of hardware, software, or services. Executive time is needed for communication and leadership activities. Funds may be needed for travel for benchmarking and meetings with customers, suppliers, and remote participants in the process. The list could go on and on. To the extent possible, management needs to allocate the needed resources and show a tangible commitment to the change process. (Remember that credibility issue?)

Insufficient Time

A second barrier that change teams face is not having time to realize the improvements. Granted, a sense of urgency is essential to the success of change projects. However, the scope of many projects is so large that it will take a long time for the results to manifest. Substantial time may also be required for overcoming organizational resistance to change. An "expert" on reengineering said that reengineering projects must be completed in six weeks to two months or they will not be successful. He must have been joking! (He wasn't.) Unless he is reengineering the simplest of processes, or throwing thousands of people at the project, that just isn't possible. Benchmarking by itself takes longer than six weeks! I advocate a "one-year" rule—select projects that can be completed in a year, or break bigger projects up into one-year increments.

Employee Fear

Losses of power, prestige, and jobs are commonplace in process improvement. A middle manager at a company going through a performance improvement process complained to me about having to give up his office as part of implementing teamwork. He said, "I waited for years to get that office, and now I have to give it up. I don't think that's fair." This man felt that he lost something through the change. However, the other employees gained something very powerful—a growing sense of equality and influence. Fear regarding loss of influence and power can be managed by talking about the rewarding experiences that replace them and the new opportunities that will open up.

Face it, how innovative are employees likely to be if it means they will lose their jobs as a result?

Fear of job loss is a different matter. Despite the evidence against it, companies do not necessarily have to lay off employees as a result of performance improvement efforts. Face it, how innovative are employees likely to be if it means they will lose their jobs as a result?

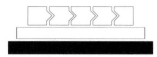

If companies can somehow create an environment where employees do not fear for their jobs, innovation and elimination of non-value-added activities (even whole departments and processes) *will increase dramatically.* "If workers know that the company will move mountains — not to mention their families and their household belongings — to help them find another position, then they're much more likely to suggest ways of doing things more efficiently." This source went on to say that one employee under a "no layoff" policy had reportedly already eliminated his own job two different times.[26]

Is it possible to downsize without layoffs? Absolutely. Maybe not in all cases, but in more than you think. Hewlett-Packard achieved a reduction in operating expenses of seven percent as a part of revenues without firing a single worker. Honeywell is completing a restructuring in which virtually nobody will be thrown out of work.[27] Capital Holding reduced its administrative staff in its Commonwealth division by 40 percent (800 people), and only 100 employees were laid off. Hills Pet Foods, a division of Colgate-Palmolive, had a similar experience. They were able to reengineer production in four plants without any layoffs.[28] What can management do to avoid layoffs? Try the following actions.

Rid yourself of poor performers before hard times strike. Good performers are far more productive than poor ones. Companies routinely wait until hard times hit and then go through an effort to weed out poor performers. Why wait? Often you can replace two poor performers with just one good one, and become a company of top performers. What a great way to downsize!

Redeploy. Most companies are not experiencing problems across their entire business. While one business unit is declining, another is growing. Instead of firing employees, redeploy them to high growth areas. Moving employees can be expensive, but the investment can bring a tenfold return of employee loyalty, creativity, and productivity.[29]

Offer selective early retirement. The key word here is selective. This can be an effective and humane tool for reducing headcount; however, it's not if you let your top talent walk out the door.

Fill idle capacity through growth. The problem may not be too much personnel. The problem may be excess capacity. How can you fill up that capacity? Can you increase revenue growth? Can you explore whole new services? Can you lease out your excess capacity?

Guarantee jobs to employees who eliminate their own jobs. This is an easy one. Guarantee employees that if their ideas result in elimination of their own job they will be given another job within the company. What a bargain!

Make employees employable. Layoffs are sometimes inevitable so companies should accept the ongoing responsibility to make their employees employable by others. This requires a corporate commitment to training, professional development, and challenging work experiences.

MEASURE PERFORMANCE AND REWARD RESULTS

Many companies fall into the trap of confusing the means with the ends. Instead of measuring tangible performance improvement *results* from their change efforts, they measure *activities* such as how many people are trained. Then the companies consider the effort successful. One of the reasons for this is that managers responsible for implementing change can "plunge wholeheartedly into these activities, relieving themselves, momentarily at least, of the burden of actually having to improve performance."[30] Several actions are available to focus on results and avoid this trap.

❖ Establish performance improvement goals.
❖ Set some goals that can be achieved in a relatively short time.
❖ Create a sense of urgency.
❖ Adopt a just-in-time approach to training—don't train until there is a tangible performance improvement objective.
❖ Focus on results—don't fall into the trap of measuring activities.
❖ Reward the results that are achieved and broadcast them to the organization.

Performance rewards have many forms. One obvious reward is economic—tie merit increases or incentive bonuses to results. However, *recognition* is also a powerful motivator that should be included as one element of the rewards. Recognition can be as little as a word of praise to an employee or as much as all-expense paid vacations awarded at company meetings. In order for recognition to effectively shape employee behavior (and ultimately the culture of an organization), it must be public and it must be fair.

This idea of fairness relates to awards given to people who don't deserve them (and the organization will know this, even if management doesn't), or awards not given to everyone who does deserve them. For instance, one company I know gave plaques to the shipping department for getting out a very large order on time. However, they omitted the accounts receivable department who worked just as hard verifying credit cards so that the order *could* ship. This experience demotivated the accounts receivable personnel. A similar problem is to give awards only to the top "x" number of performers (that is, the three people whose process improvements saved the company the most dollars). This may result in exceptional performance going unrewarded. A better approach is to reward everyone who achieves a certain level of performance, even if it means rewarding a whole lot more people (and hopefully it does). After all, isn't it better to motivate 100 people to save a million dollars each than three people to save $5 million each?

TPM Part 2

Create Performance Improvement Capability

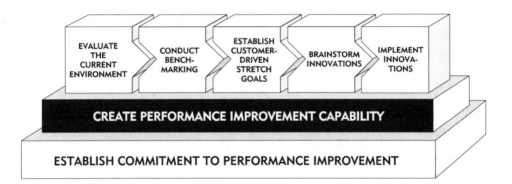

| EVALUATE THE CURRENT ENVIRONMENT | CONDUCT BENCH-MARKING | ESTABLISH CUSTOMER-DRIVEN STRETCH GOALS | BRAINSTORM INNOVATIONS | IMPLEMENT INNOVA-TIONS |

CREATE PERFORMANCE IMPROVEMENT CAPABILITY

ESTABLISH COMMITMENT TO PERFORMANCE IMPROVEMENT

CARING FOR THE GOLDEN GOOSE

7

Committing to Employee Education

Training is everything. The peach was once a bitter almond; cauliflower is nothing but cabbage with a college education.

— Mark Twain

It isn't enough that people understand and accept the need to change. They need the skills necessary to work together to brainstorm innovations, solve problems, and implement the solutions. Part 2 of Total Process Management completes the foundation section of the methodology. It provides the skills to complement the organizational will established in TPM Part 1.

This part of the TPM methodology answers the question, *How do we obtain the skills needed to implement change?* Topics covered in this section include:

- ❖ Corporate Commitment to Learning
- ❖ Process Improvement Principles (Chapter 8)
- ❖ Problem Analysis Tools and Techniques (Chapter 9)
- ❖ Creative Brainstorming (Chapter 10)

Employees must first understand how to make processes better before they can improve performance. They learn this through the *process improvement principles* and *creative brainstorming*. In the Total Process Management methodology, these skills are applied in Part 6, Brainstorm Innovations. However, it is useful to understand the principles even while documenting the current environment to alert employees to *opportunities* for improvement.

Understanding how to identify and prioritize the underlying causes of problems is a critical skill for effective process improvement. Employees learn this through the *problem analysis tools and techniques*. These skills are useful through every stage of the process improvement cycle. They are particularly helpful in documenting the current environment (TPM, Part 3) and in focus group brainstorming (TPM, Part 6).

CORPORATE COMMITMENT TO LEARNING

Shame on corporate America! Companies in America invest almost nothing in the education of their employees. In hard times, it is the first thing to go — ironically, at the very time that it is needed most. Downsizing companies eliminate employee training with the hope of "becoming

lean and mean, and end up lean and lame."[1] Here are the facts. American companies spend a yearly average of $400 per employee on training. For that $400 each employee gets about 20 hours of training — half of one week. It's worse for hourly wage earners. They get around $225 a year for a whopping 16 hours of training — two workdays out of 250![2]

Why train your employees? Without training you are killing the golden goose. You are benefiting from the efforts of your employees and at the same time limiting their ability to continue to produce results. How are employees to continue to contribute in a changing environment without adequate education to keep them abreast of the changes? Stephen Covey calls this *P/PC balance.* "*P* stands for *production* of desired results, the golden eggs. *PC* stands for production capability, the ability or asset that produces the golden egg."[3] His point is that you have to balance caring for the goose (your employees) with harvesting the golden eggs (your employees' production). When you achieve P/PC balance, your effectiveness is maximized.

> *Thinking to get at once all the gold the goose could give, he killed it and opened it only to find nothing.*
>
> *— Aesop*

A company's investment in employee education can be viewed as the pyramid of value shown in Figure 7.1. In this model, performance excellence (every company's goal) rests on top of the foundation of employee education. No education — no performance excellence. It's also important for companies to recognize the difference between training and education. Training teaches people how to do something. Education teaches people why to do it. Companies will never achieve worker empowerment without educating employees on the why's of business.

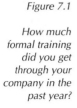

Figure 7.1

How much formal training did you get through your company in the past year?

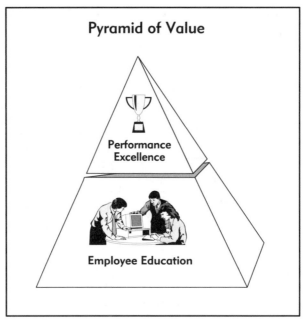

Pyramid of Value

Performance Excellence

Employee Education

One reason corporate America is reluctant to spend money on training is because it is hard to measure the benefits of the training. Few companies are able to estimate potential benefits from training, nor can they evaluate the results from training. One expert estimates that as much as 50% of the dollars spent on training is wasted.[4] It is fair to ask employees to invest in their training, too, since their benefit from the training goes beyond just the current corporate environment. In some cases, companies ask that their employees take the training in part or entirely during non-work hours. Other companies have employees

sign a document requiring them to repay the training costs if they leave the company within a fixed time (usually two years).

One solution that many companies are turning to is just-in-time (JIT) training. For instance, Rubbermaid, Johnson and Johnson, and Herman Miller now do their training through teams that are assigned to tasks.[5] With JIT training, companies provide training to employees only when they have an immediate and specific application of the material. In this way, it is easier to evaluate the results of the training, and the employees retain more of the material because it is reinforced immediately. Analog Devices is one company that has adopted JIT training. They started with an experiment where half of a group of 900 employees was trained in a classroom setting and the other half was trained as teams on the job. The result was that less than 40% of the first group claimed they had put the training to work while 80% of those trained as teams did.[6]

Many companies are turning to just-in-time training.

Just-in-time training is particularly effective in rolling out change management methodologies. This is especially so considering the cost of these efforts. One study by Towers and Perrin estimates the training bill for a company of 13,000 employees could run as much as $12 million![7] For expenditures of that magnitude, it is essential that companies obtain an appropriate return on their investment. Total Process Management is perfectly suited to JIT training. Each of the subjects discussed in this chapter can be presented as stand-alone training courses at the specific time they are needed and can be applied immediately. Consider the following example.

> Your company wants to implement process value improvement throughout the company, but has funds for only a limited roll out of the methodology. You can start by selecting a motivated workgroup with a track record for innovation and self-directed change. Teach this group the seven-part TPM methodology. As their first assignment, and to apply their training, ask them to identify an improvement opportunity. When they have one identified, teach the group the problem analysis tools and problem-solving techniques and have them evaluate the causes of the problem. After this is completed, teach the group the process improvement principles and creative brainstorming techniques. Then have them brainstorm innovations to improve the process. Have the team implement the innovations. Last, have this team go out and teach two other teams the same material in the same way. What a great way to reinforce the training!

The next three chapters discuss the process improvement principles, problem-solving and analysis techniques, and creative brainstorming. There are many other base skills that are required for successful change that are not included here due to the sheer volume of material involved. These include teamwork, managing as a coach, worker empowerment, and many other topics. The key point of Part 2 of the TPM methodology is that certain core skills must be developed for change to succeed. However, the specific skills that are needed will vary from company to company.

THIRTY-TWO
WAYS TO SHINE

8

The Process Improvement Principles

"There is another and a better world."
— *August Friedrich Ferdinand von Kotzebue*

There are a lot of ways in which to improve processes. In this chapter, 32 process improvement principles that have proven to be effective at one time or another in process improvement projects are discussed. These are grouped into the eight categories shown in Figure 8.1. The groupings are for convenience only, to help in understanding and remembering the principles. Most of the principles are interrelated and should be used in conjunction with others from different categories.

Figure 8.1

*TPM has 32
process
improvement
principles
grouped into
eight categories.*

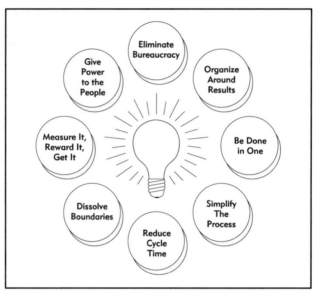

Process Improvement Principles:

* ❖ Eliminate duplicate activities
* ❖ Combine related activities
* ❖ Eliminate reviews and approvals
* ❖ Reduce preparation
* ❖ Outsource
* ❖ Eliminate transporting
* ❖ Eliminate filing
* ❖ Organize multi-functional teams
* ❖ Design cellular workplaces
* ❖ Create case managers

- ❖ Centralize/decentralize — hybridize
- ❖ Create quality at the source
- ❖ Mistake proof
- ❖ Eliminate inspections
- ❖ Input at the source
- ❖ Create case workers
- ❖ Change the order of activities
- ❖ Create multiple process versions
- ❖ Standardize on best practices
- ❖ Use smaller batch sizes
- ❖ Implement demand pull
- ❖ Process in parallel
- ❖ Dissolve vertical boundaries
- ❖ Dissolve horizontal boundaries
- ❖ Dissolve external boundaries
- ❖ Measure the right things
- ❖ Reward the right things
- ❖ Walk the talk
- ❖ Involve employees
- ❖ Establish a teamwork culture
- ❖ Make the customer boss
- ❖ Don't pass the monkey

ELIMINATE BUREAUCRACY

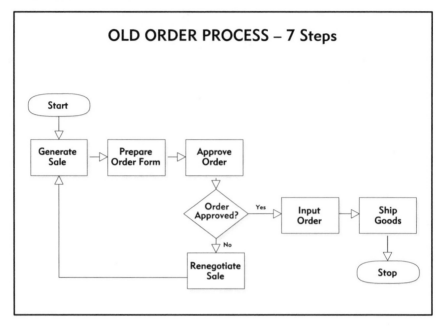

- ◆ Eliminate duplicate activities
- ◆ Combine related activities
- ◆ Eliminate reviews and approvals
- ◆ Reduce preparation
- ◆ Outsource
- ◆ Eliminate transporting
- ◆ Eliminate filing

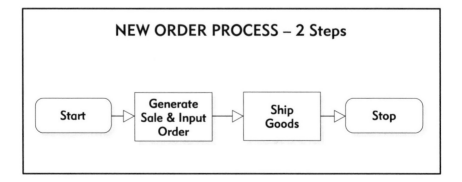

Eliminate Bureaucracy

Eliminate Duplicate Activities. Duplicate activities are pervasive. Duplication usually derives from lack of trust in the process due to absence of quality at the source. Do things once and do them right — eliminate duplication!

Combine Related Activities. Tasks that have close association, such as generating a sale and entering the order, can be combined. Segmentation of tasks creates delays, errors, and extra handling time.

> *"Less is more."*
> — *Robert Browning*

Eliminate Reviews and Approvals. In most companies, many documents require three or more authorizations. When there are multiple approvals, who is accountable? Limit approvals to one person and only for important transactions. Then there is no question who is accountable and cycle time is greatly improved.

Reduce Preparation. When a task starts with "Prepare . . ." or has anything to do with a form, an opportunity for process improvement exists. Customers do not value the time spent *preparing* for tasks. They only value the time spent *doing* them!

Outsource. If you cannot execute a process or activity better *and* less expensively than you can purchase the service, consider outsourcing. When you "have your act together," then bring it back in-house. Let's get competitive — that means service processes too!

Eliminate Transporting. Mailing or moving work products means delays. It also requires money to pay the movers, space to accumulate stacks of stuff, and start-up time to determine what you have. Move people together, use common information systems, or combine the tasks, but stop shuffling work around!

ORGANIZE AROUND RESULTS

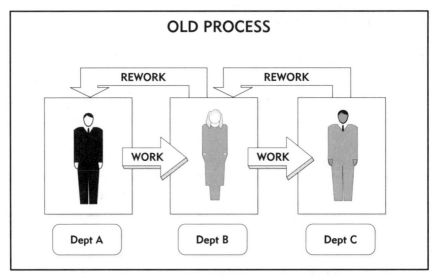

- ◆ Organize multi-functional teams
- ◆ Design cellular workplaces
- ◆ Create case managers
- ◆ Centralize/decentralize — hybridize

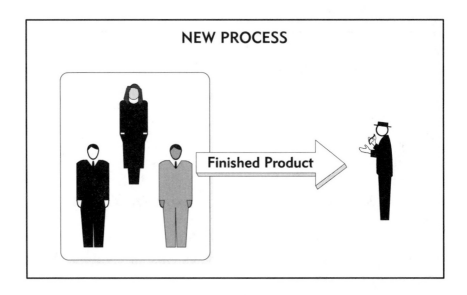

Organize Around Results

Organize Multi-Functional Teams. Typically, companies are organized into functional departments. Information and work products move in lurching hand-offs from one department to the next. Disagreements are handled by sending the problem up the chain of command, across the top, down the other side and then back again. A process organized functionally is expensive, slow, and inflexible — hardly the definition of a customer-centered process!

One approach to this problem is to create multi-functional teams. This requires that workers from all departments involved in a process be assigned as teams. The team is responsible for the entire output, not just a component. This focuses the various functional groups on the customer need (the output) and not on departmental agendas (turf battles).

Design Cellular Workplaces. Physical separation of the people involved in a process will result in batching and transporting work products to the next station. It will delay communication or cause poor communication. The opportunity for error will enter the process. An effective solution is to move the people involved in the process to a group setting to create a cellular workplace. In this scenario, several work teams are formed, and each group is responsible for an entire work product.

Create Case Managers. When multi-functional process teams are impractical due to size, complexity, or resource constraints, a case manager may be assigned. This person is the single contact point between the customer and the work groups, and acts in place of a multi-functional team. The case manager has responsibility for delivering results to the customer, and the information and authority to do so.

Centralize/Decentralize — Hybridize. Today we are centralized. Tomorrow we will be decentralized. Next week we will be centralized again. Sound familiar? This occurs because each organizational approach has legitimate advantages. However, you can use today's advanced technologies to take advantage of the best of both. For example, you can electronically link the small, responsive decentralized operations with the centralized processes that offer economies of scale. Hybridize!

BE DONE IN ONE

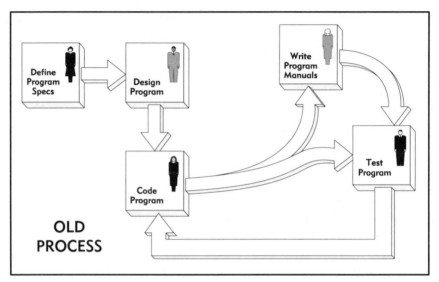

OLD PROCESS

- ◆ Create quality at the source
- ◆ Mistake proof
- ◆ Eliminate inspections
- ◆ Input at the source
- ◆ Create case workers

Define Program Specs
Design Program
Code Program
Write Program Manuals
Test Program

NEW PROCESS

Be Done in One

The object of Be Done in One is to complete the product without it being handed off to other people or departments during the process.

Create Quality at the Source. In improving processes, look for activities such as inspection and quality assurance as a signal that the work did not start with quality. The goal of the process improvement team is to design the new process so that the work can only be done the correct way. Quality does not start with the product — it starts with the process that creates the product.

Mistake Proof. One technique for improving quality at the source is to create mistake-proof processes. Examples of these processes include computer input programs with sophisticated validations, self-correcting machinery, and self-totaling forms.

Eliminate Inspections. In addition to building quality in at the source, the process improvement team should try to eliminate inspections. Usually, inspections are performed "just-in-case" there is a problem. The cost in cycle time, personnel, and exception processing far exceeds the savings derived from the few problems actually found.

Input at the Source. "I'm a salesperson, not a data entry clerk!" This was the answer once heard about why salespersons in a Fortune 1000 company filled out forms instead of inputting orders directly into a computer. Is this justification for inefficient and costly processes? The process improvement team should eliminate data entry and input preparation. Sophisticated technology can be leveraged to make this a relatively painless effort for the initiator. Let's put an end to the lament, "That's not my job!"

Create Case Workers. One of the most powerful approaches available for process improvement is the concept of a multi-functional (case) worker. Using this approach, workers are trained with all of the skills required to complete the entire process. In addition to creating a more interesting and rewarding job, you eliminate errors, miscommunication, delays, and bureaucracy.

SIMPLIFY THE PROCESS

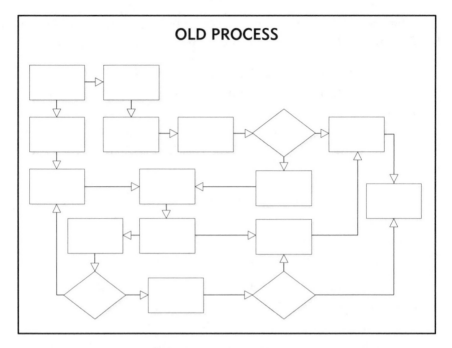

- ◆ Change the order of activities
- ◆ Create multiple process versions
- ◆ Standardize on best practices

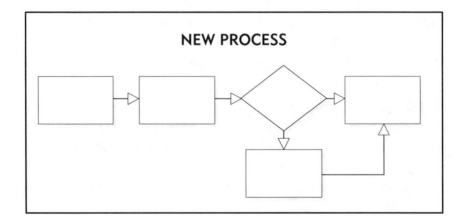

Simplify the Process

Processes are often unnecessarily complex. This is a result of the way most processes evolve. When problems crop up in the process, hastily formulated short-term solutions are applied. The problem seems to be fixed so we move on to the next raging fire. Another short-term fix is applied to that problem. Soon our short-term fixes have become long-term solutions. Since nobody can remember why they were put in place, everyone is afraid to change them. Over the years, these patchwork solutions pile up layer upon layer.

> *Our life is frittered away by detail. . . . Simplify, simplify.*
> — Henry David Thoreau

Change the Order of Activities. In some circumstances, processes are made unnecessarily complex because of the order in which the activities are conducted. Consider the example of documents that are received in one place, sent to another place for approval, and then returned to the original location. Simplify and streamline this process by having the document sent *first* to the approver and then to the final destination. This would eliminate several steps and increase the cycle time substantially.

Create Multiple Process Versions. Most processes have only one version — the "one size fits all" model. Unlike humanity, not all transactions are created equal. Some are small and simple; others are very large and complex. Transaction volumes can vary widely. In a "one size fits all" approach the simple transactions are treated the same as the large complex ones, and end up taking just as long and costing just as much to process. Fit the process to the transaction — have multiple versions!

Standardize on Best Practices. Many of the principles already presented are powerful tools for simplifying processes. These principles include eliminate redundancy, combine fragmented tasks, input at the source, and create case workers. Once a process has been simplified, standardize on it. Document the process and teach it to the other employees so that everyone's performance can benefit from the best practice.

REDUCE CYCLE TIME

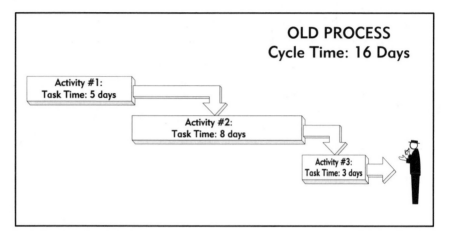

- ◆ Use small batch sizes
- ◆ Implement demand pull
- ◆ Process in parallel

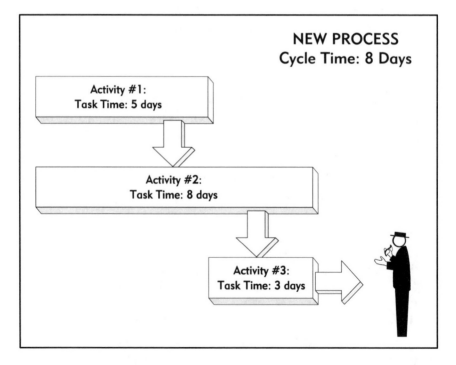

Reduce Cycle Time

Cycle time, the time that it takes a transaction to move through the entire process, is critical in today's "speed is life" business environment. Most of the principles already discussed contribute to reduced cycle times. Several additional approaches are discussed below.

Use Small Batch Sizes. Traditionally, transactions (whether they are invoices or end products) are moved through the process in large batches. At any time, there can be multiple batches at any particular work station along the process. This reduces the visibility of individual transactions, and creates a large amount of work-in-progress that must be stored somewhere. It slows the discovery of breakdowns in the process, and contributes to rework that greatly increases the time an individual transaction spends in the process. Not a pretty sight!

To make the process better, implement small batch sizes with fewer transactions. Just one transaction is best of all. Small batch sizes smooth work flow throughout the process and eliminate bottlenecks. Stress on the system will be reduced and work-in-progress will be reduced. Visibility will increase and costs due to poor quality will be reduced. Cycle time will be drastically reduced by small batch sizes.

Implement Demand Pull. This principle works in conjunction with small batch sizes to reduce cycle time and smooth the process work flow. Currently, we often operate under the "supply push" method, which means that whatever work we complete is pushed to the next work station whether they are ready for it or not. What happens on the receiving end? Frequently, the work just stacks up until someone can get to it, and then you have the same problem that is caused by large batch sizes. The solution is to use a "demand pull" system. In this scenario, work is not passed on until the next work station asks for it. This model is used in the highly successful just-in-time manufacturing approach.

Process in Parallel. Many processes align tasks serially with one starting only after the previous task is completed. An effective method of reducing cycle time is to conduct activities concurrently (parallel processes). This approach requires frequent communication between the teams, but can reduce overall cycle time dramatically.

DISSOLVE BOUNDARIES

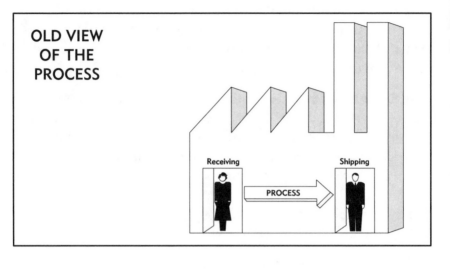

OLD VIEW OF THE PROCESS

- ◆ Dissolve vertical boundaries
- ◆ Dissolve horizontal boundaries
- ◆ Dissolve external boundaries

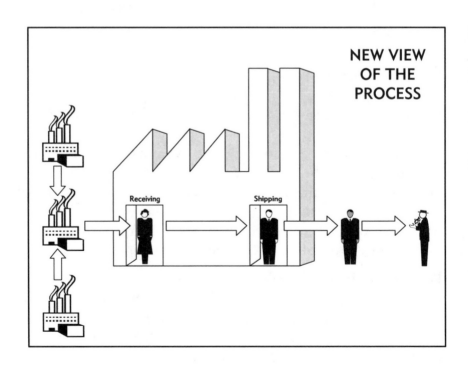

NEW VIEW OF THE PROCESS

Dissolve Boundaries

Many companies are characterized by boundaries. Boundaries to the left. Boundaries to the right. Even boundaries above us. Companies who want to become world-class must dissolve these boundaries.

Dissolve Vertical Boundaries. Hierarchical organizations are inherently boundary-full. Bosses are bosses, and everyone else isn't. That point is reinforced daily. What makes for vertical boundaries? Differences in power and access to information are two key elements of command and control hierarchies. To dissolve vertical boundaries, companies must remove layers of management to reduce the psychological distance between front-line workers and top management. Information must flow freely between the top and bottom of the organization. Front-line worker compensation must begin to mirror that of top management—tying their compensation to the performance of the company and not just to their own performance.

Dissolve Horizontal Boundaries. Walls between groups include those separating functional groups, geographic groups, and product groups. Regardless of the type of wall, they have the same effect—they decrease communication and cooperation, increase hand-offs and opportunities for errors, and increase cycle time. To dissolve these boundaries, companies can structure the organization around processes, create multi-functional teams, and promote an understanding of the inter-relatedness of business processes.

Dissolve External Boundaries. Processes do not begin at the receiving dock and end at the shipping dock. They begin somewhere beyond our supplier's supplier and end with whomever our customers serve. Enormous advantages in cost, cycle time, and quality improvements accrue to companies that optimize this overall process. However, it cannot be done by sourcing from the low-cost provider or by ignoring the customer. We must create true value chains that run across multiple companies. Outsource some processes to suppliers who can do it better or cheaper. Likewise, have your customer outsource to your company the activities that you can do better. Dissolve customer/supplier boundaries, and reap the benefits!

MEASURE IT, REWARD IT, GET IT

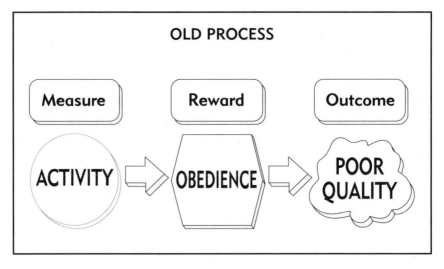

- ◆ Measure the right things
- ◆ Reward the right things
- ◆ Walk the talk
- ◆ Involve employees

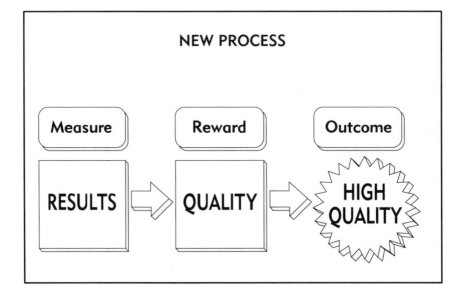

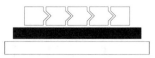

Measure It, Reward It, Get it

Effective measurement systems and rewards are essential to achieving performance goals. Unfortunately, these points are poorly understood and inconsistently applied.

Measure the Right Things. Very often the *means* is confused with the *end* — doing activities is not the same as delivering results. For instance, workaholics work many hours more than most. Time after time these people are pointed out as the "stars" of the organization. The question is what are they producing with those long hours? Is it better to work long or work smart? Total Quality Management programs often fail because managers are measured on how many people are trained on TQM, rather than improvements that result from the training. Measure results, not activities.

Reward the Right Things. In process improvement, the ultimate goal is to improve customer satisfaction. Are employees rewarded on customer satisfaction? How much of their compensation is tied to making sure the customer is happy?

Most companies measure one thing and reward another. For example, many companies today promote teamwork, but compensate employees solely on individual contribution. What is the motivation to work as a team member when commission is based only on sales? People do what is rewarded, so reward what is really wanted.

Walk the Talk. Behavior modeling is one of the strongest learning mechanisms in humans. Employees will look to their leaders for what they do, not what they say. If managers ask for honest feedback, but promote only those people with positive things to say, soon everyone will say only positive things. Do what you say and your employees will too.

Involve Employees. Ownership is a powerful motivator. If you involve employees in establishing performance measures and rewards, measuring their own performance and initiating improvements, they often will surprise you by exceeding your expectations.

GIVE POWER TO THE PEOPLE

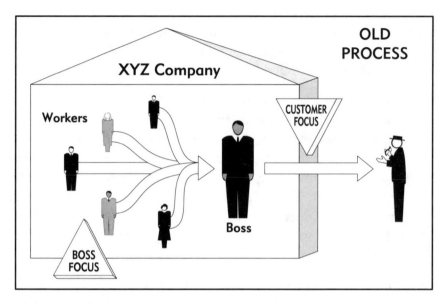

- ◆ Establish a teamwork culture
- ◆ Make the customer boss
- ◆ Don't pass the monkey

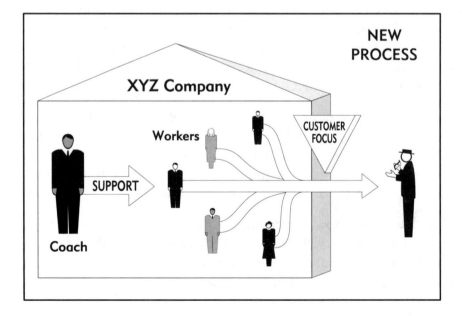

Give Power to the People

Command and control management systems are dead, but many companies just do not know it yet. How will a traditional hierarchical, bureaucratic company compete when the next company has fewer layers of management, better and faster communication, and thousands of problem solvers instead of a few hundred?

Establish a Teamwork Culture. Teams are more effective and efficient than individuals working separately for most business activities. Contrary to popular opinion, teams do not suppress individual talents and excellence but leverage these talents for group successes. Frequently, top performers do so at the expense of others in the organization. Teams and group goals eliminate this problem while maximizing and celebrating the individual's contribution. Teamwork has to be a shared value that comes down from the top. Also, effective teamwork requires training and reinforcement.

Make the Customer Boss. Inwardly focused companies care more about making the boss happy than the customer. World-class companies want to make the customer happy. What then is the new role of the boss? Their new role is to coach multi-functional, self-directed teams to achieve goals that have been set by the customer. With multiple functions working together, employees and teams making their own decisions, and customers setting the goals, companies will need fewer layers of management and will operate both more efficiently and effectively.

Don't Pass the Monkey. Sadly, the resistance to empowering workers does not come only from panic-stricken middle managers. It also comes from the workers themselves. Traditionally, employees have gone to the boss, handed over the problem (the "monkey"), and gone back to their work. They were relieved to have passed the monkey. No more. In empowered companies, managers don't take the monkey. Their role is to coach and support. It is each worker's responsibility to solve the problem and satisfy the customer.

CHARLES DARWIN WAS RIGHT

9

Problem Analysis Tools and Techniques

*"Man is a tool using animal. . . .
Without tools he is nothing, with tools
he is all."*

—Carlyle

Charles Darwin was right—man does rely on the use of tools to advance mankind. At the doorstep of the 21st century, we still rely on tools. Only now the tools aren't axes and spears (for most of us); the tools are computers, software, and mathematical techniques. Two topics are discussed in this chapter. The first is identifying the problem that needs to be solved. Then we discuss a number of analysis tools and techniques that can be used to determine the underlying causes of the problem. The next chapter, on creative brainstorming, discusses how to generate alternative solutions for the causes of the problem.

What is the problem? In many instances, people begin problem analysis without first developing a clear understanding of the real problem. We often find that our disagreements result from arguing about *different understandings*

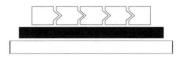

of the problem. How will we ever agree on a solution if we aren't even working on the same problem? One way in which this can be avoided is to define the problem as a three-part statement as follows:

1. What is the current condition?

2. What is the impact?

3. What is the desired improvement?

An example of a poorly defined problem is shown below. As you can see, it doesn't meet *any* of the three criteria listed above, but it probably looks familiar to many of you as a typical problem statement.

"We don't have enough service representatives during peak hours."

That really isn't a statement of the problem so much as a statement of the solution needed. We can restate the problem using the three-part statement approach to give us a much better problem statement.

❖ *Current condition:* At times our customers are waiting on hold more than ten minutes.

❖ *Impact:* As a result, many of them are hanging up or voicing dissatisfaction about the wait.

❖ *Desired Improvement:* Customer wait time should never exceed two minutes.

Putting the three parts together, our new problem statement becomes:

> *At times our customers are waiting on hold more than ten minutes. As a result, many of them are hanging up or voicing dissatisfaction about the wait. Customer wait time should never exceed two minutes.*

With a clearly stated problem, we can begin analyzing the underlying causes. There are a number of effective analytical techniques for identifying underlying problem causes. Some of the techniques are discussed below. However, the process improvement team may first need to narrow down the number of possible causes to a manageable few. One tool for this is multi-voting. Multi-voting can be used before or after the problem analysis tools.

Multi-voting is a technique used to narrow down the potential causes of a problem to the top few. There are several steps involved in multi-voting.

❖ Brainstorm possible causes, and display them where everyone can see.

❖ Conduct a series of votes to narrow the list. Everyone can vote for as many causes as they want.

❖ Display a list with only the causes that received the top number of votes.

❖ Conduct a second vote. Each person has half as many votes as there are causes.

❖ Narrow the list again and repeat the voting process until you have an acceptable number of causes.

Problem-Solving and Analysis "Tool Kit"

Process Flowcharts & Maps

Pareto Charts

Cause-and-Effect Diagrams

Histograms

Check Sheets

Run Charts

Scatter Diagrams

Control Charts

Process Cost Analysis

Cycle Time Analysis

Total Process Management uses a number of tools for identifying and evaluating areas for improvement. As with any tool, it is important that the tool fit the need, and not be used indiscriminately. Figure 9.1 lists the key problem-solving and analysis tools used in TPM. In many cases, the tools will be used in conjunction with one or more of the other tools.

PROCESS FLOWCHARTS AND MAPS

In Total Process Management, the fundamental tools for evaluating and understanding business are *process flowcharts* and a particular kind of flowchart called a *process map*. A process flowchart is the basic unit of documentation required to understand and manage the effectiveness of business processes. Process flowcharts include inputs to the process and their sources, outputs from the process and their destinations, and all processing steps required to create the outputs. The most widely used and understood symbols are shown in Figure 9.2. However, any flowchart symbols can be used, as long as everyone uses them consistently.

Here are some of the benefits of developing and maintaining process flowcharts:

❖ Sufficiently detailed process flowcharts can replace traditional documentation done in outline format using word processing software. With flowcharting software, processing rules and exceptions can be entered into text fields within the shapes on the process flowchart.

❖ Flowcharting software, such as ABC FlowCharter, provides a graphic representation of the process, making it easier for employees to grasp how their job fits into the larger context of the business.

❖ Process flowcharts are an excellent tool for surfacing process inefficiencies.

❖ Effective process flowcharting can fulfill the documentation requirement of quality standards such as ISO 9000.

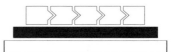

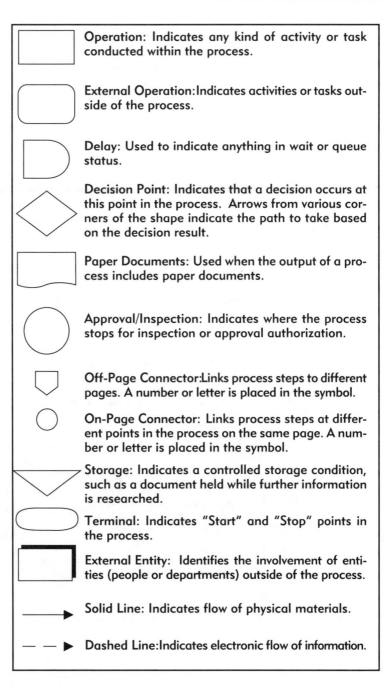

Figure 9.2

These are the most commonly used process flowchart symbols, but you can use any symbols as long as they are used consistently.

Operation: Indicates any kind of activity or task conducted within the process.

External Operation: Indicates activities or tasks outside of the process.

Delay: Used to indicate anything in wait or queue status.

Decision Point: Indicates that a decision occurs at this point in the process. Arrows from various corners of the shape indicate the path to take based on the decision result.

Paper Documents: Used when the output of a process includes paper documents.

Approval/Inspection: Indicates where the process stops for inspection or approval authorization.

Off-Page Connector: Links process steps to different pages. A number or letter is placed in the symbol.

On-Page Connector: Links process steps at different points in the process on the same page. A number or letter is placed in the symbol.

Storage: Indicates a controlled storage condition, such as a document held while further information is researched.

Terminal: Indicates "Start" and "Stop" points in the process.

External Entity: Identifies the involvement of entities (people or departments) outside of the process.

Solid Line: Indicates flow of physical materials.

Dashed Line: Indicates electronic flow of information.

Businesses need to develop and maintain process flow-charts for every process in the company. Everyone who participates in the process (referred to as *process members*) should understand the entire process and how his or her job fits into it. The process flowchart should be posted either on a wall or on a computer network where all the process members can review it periodically. Update any changes to the actual working of the process on the flowchart immediately. Communicate these changes to all process members. This is an essential component of institutionalizing the improvements made in processes so that old inefficiencies and errors aren't repeated.

Each person who participates in a process should understand the entire process and how his or her job fits into it.

The first step in understanding a company's business processes is to develop a top-level map of the processes (called

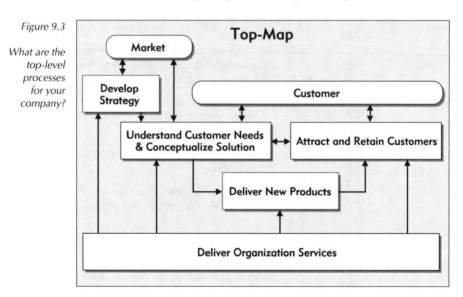

Figure 9.3

What are the top-level processes for your company?

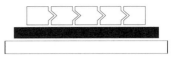

a top-map) as shown in Figure 9.3. An effective top-map is something employees can quickly understand and which fits their image of the company. Coincidentally, the top-map is a supportive tool that allows restructuring your company around processes. In the *horizontal company* each top-level process is assigned to a senior executive, not to a functional department.

The most effective way to develop enterprise-wide flow-charts is to start with the top-map and develop increasingly detailed process flowcharts hierarchically. Software is available that lets you link flowcharts. Using linked flowcharts, you can be assured that the relationships among processes fit into the overall business context and that there are no processes unaccounted for. This also helps to validate the top-map. The process flowcharting can be continued until the desired level of detail is achieved.

Process maps are flowcharts that capture substantially more information. Besides the information in a process flow-chart, process maps include certain characteristics that further define the process. Process maps can be used instead of the process flowcharts for enterprise-wide process documentation. Although the additional information is useful for ongoing process value improvement, these maps take longer to develop and require more frequent changes. Many companies reserve process mapping for periodic improvement projects (such as process reinvention or process improvement workgroup projects), and use process flowcharting everyday. Another approach is to develop process maps at a higher point in the process hierarchy where there are fewer operations. The process maps at a more summarized level are easier to develop and maintain with the additional information included.

Any shape on the process map where action is taken is called an *operation*. Some or all the following information can be captured for each operation:

❖ *Responsibility for performing the operation* — Usually the job title.

❖ *Operation description* — Brief description of the action taken.

❖ *Cost/Resources consumed* — Cost per unit, or number of work hours or full-time equivalent people required for the task over a fixed time.

❖ *Activity Time* — Time required to actually perform the task.

❖ *Elapsed Time* — Entire time a unit is being processed, including wait time.

❖ *Volume measures* — Units or transactions processed (remember to identify the transaction type).

❖ *Activity mode* — On-line, batch, or manual.

❖ *Performance Measures* — Measures for current performance expectations.

❖ *Frequency* — How often the activity is performed.

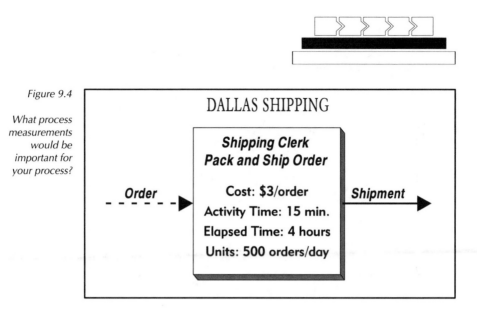

Figure 9.4

What process measurements would be important for your process?

DALLAS SHIPPING

Order

Shipping Clerk
Pack and Ship Order

Cost: $3/order
Activity Time: 15 min.
Elapsed Time: 4 hours
Units: 500 orders/day

Shipment

Each arrow entering an operation should be labeled with the material and/or information being input. Arrows leaving operations should be labeled with the material and/or information being output from the operation. A sample process map operation and corresponding metrics are shown in Figure 9.4.

Deployment process maps are the most commonly used type of process map. These are used to show individuals, job titles, or departments across the top or down the side of the flowchart. The opposite axis represents time. Process symbols are shown in relation to the department where the work is performed. I prefer showing departments down the left side with time moving horizontally. For large processes (and most are), a process map can cover 10 to 20 square feet or more. When displayed on a wall, a vertical chart will have you on your knees to see the last of the process map. A horizontal map allows you to simply move around the wall. A sample deployment process map is shown in Figure 9.5.

Figure 9.5

Deployment flowcharts show process flow across several departments.

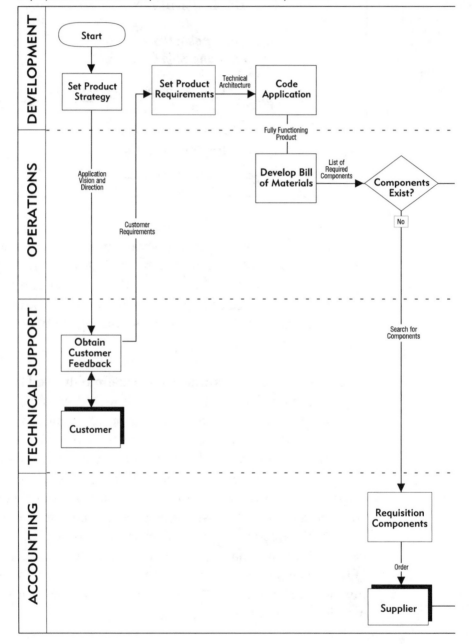

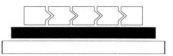

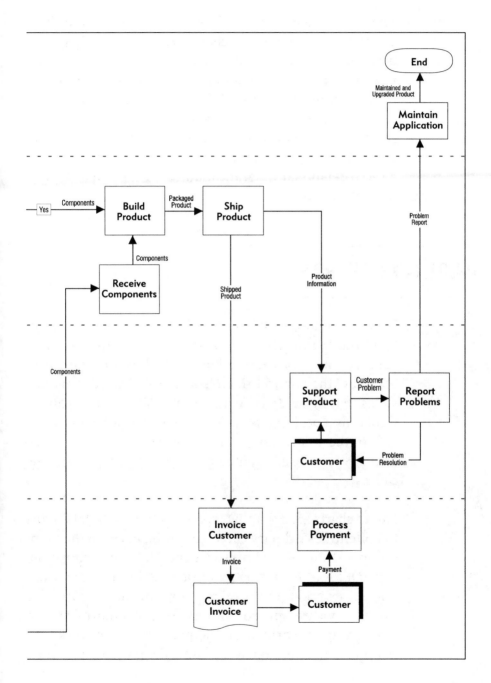

There are several other kinds of process flowcharts as well. These include hierarchy charts, Warnier-Orr diagrams, network diagrams, bubble charts, and relational diagrams. It is important that the tool fit the need. The process improvement team may find that in certain circumstances one type of flowchart may be better than others. For instance, documenting heavy interaction between humans and machines or information systems may be more suited to a relational diagram than to a traditional deployment flowchart.

PARETO CHARTS

Vilfredo Pareto, a 19th-century Italian economist, formulated the Maldistribution of Wealth Rule. Joseph Juran later redefined the rule into the *Pareto Principle*. Many people know the Pareto Principle as the 80-20 rule. This rule states that most effects come from relatively few causes. Generally speaking, 80% of any result is attributable to 20% of the contributing activity. For example, out of 100 errors, 80 can be eliminated by correcting only 20% of the causes.

Pareto charts are a graphic representation of the 80-20 rule that identifies primary causes of problems with the highest opportunities for improvement. This is an *enormously important* tool for prioritizing process improvement opportunities and for maximizing improvement efforts. For process value improvement, it can ensure that a workgroup is working on the most important problem. In process reinvention, it can show the project team those

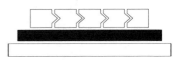

errors that should be focused on to provide the greatest overall improvement.

To create Pareto charts, information about any characteristic of a process is accumulated and represented in a graphic format. The value with the most frequent occurrence is shown as a column on the left of the chart. Successively less frequent occurrences are ordered in descending sequence moving to the right. Relatively insignificant occurrences can be grouped into a final column called "other," or omitted from the chart entirely. Sometimes it is useful to display occurrences on the left y-axis of the

Figure 9.6

Pareto charts identify primary causes of problems with the highest opportunities for improvement.

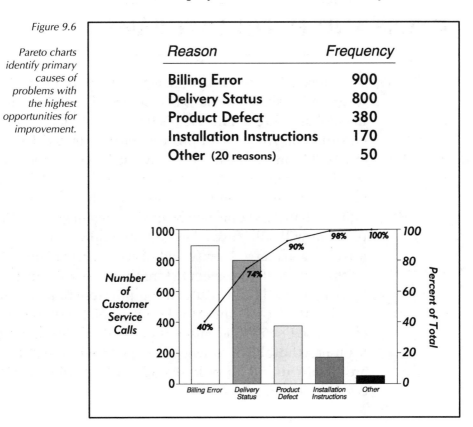

chart, and percentage of the total on a y-axis at the right of the chart. A line can be drawn starting from the first column adding the percentage increase from each subsequent column until 100% is reached.

A sample Pareto chart is shown in Figure 9.6. In this example, the reasons customers give for calling customer support are prioritized. The top two categories of concern are billing and delivery. The focus for remedial efforts can be on these areas.

CAUSE-AND-EFFECT DIAGRAMS

The cause-and-effect diagram, also known as a fishbone diagram or Ishikawa chart, is a powerful problem-solving tool used to examine factors that may influence a given situation. Along with process flowcharts and Pareto charts, it is one of the most widely used analysis tools. In problem solving, people frequently identify only the most obvious causes of a problem and target them for correction. Soon these people will be meeting again because the problem will still exist. They did not address the other, less obvious causes. A cause-and-effect diagram highlights all the causes of a problem before trying to solve it. This tool can be used to structure the output from brainstorming or as the focal point of the brainstorming. Although it can be used by individuals, it is particularly effective for team-based problem solving. Cause-and-effect diagrams are equally useful for process improvement and for process reinvention.

Cause-and-effect diagrams can be used in a wide variety of analyses. In one case, a company used a cause-and-effect diagram to help better understand why their cost of goods sold (COGS) was running high. Through the diagram, the product team was able to understand the broad range of factors that cumulatively affect the COGS. Individually, no single increase in component cost was significant. When decisions were reached to increase the cost of components in a number of different places, the cumulative effect was to substantially increase the overall cost of goods sold. Using the diagram as a basis, the team was able to rethink the individual cost decisions and reduce the product cost of goods sold.

The example in Figure 9.7 regards a customer service department's inability to answer customer requests on the first call. The cause-and-effect diagram begins with a clear statement of the problem or desired effect. This is placed in a box at the right of the diagram and becomes the effect. Draw a horizontal line out from the box to the left, forming the central line of the diagram (the spine of the "fish"). Now identify the major causes of the effect. These can be anything—in our example, the four causes are skills, procedures, information systems, and authority. Draw these as boxes at the end of diagonal lines (leaning left) drawn from the central line (the "spines" of the fish). From these, begin one at a time with the major causes and identify their primary causes. Document them on lines leading from the "spines." Add sub-causes to these until enough detail has been reached. The same cause can be repeated at multiple places in the diagram if appropriate. Ultimately you will have a complete list of causes and sub-causes.

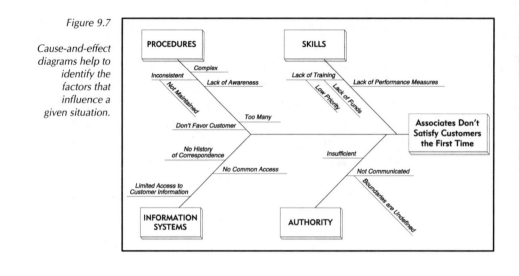

Figure 9.7

*Cause-and-effect
diagrams help to
identify the
factors that
influence a
given situation.*

HISTOGRAMS

A histogram is a graphic representation of variations in a set of data. The object is to view trends in variation in large sets of data values that otherwise might not be easy to detect. Histograms are based on the knowledge that all variations have a pattern (called distributions), and that the pattern can reveal much about the underlying variations. These distributions have three characteristics to evaluate: center, width, and shape. The center is the expected or average data value. The distribution could ordinarily be expected to vary evenly around the center (a bell curve or normal distribution). When it doesn't, and either is too wide, skewed to one side, or has an odd distribution, there may be underlying problems that should be investigated and corrected. Histograms are generally more useful for process improvement than for process reinvention.

Create a histogram by developing a table of data representing variations, such as the variation in the length of customer service calls. Group the values by some increment (one minute in our example). The center value (expected call length) is ten minutes. The occurrences in each increment from the center are counted and represented on the graph as a vertical bar. The height of each bar is the number of occurrences for that increment. All the bars are added to the graph until there is a complete distribution. The distribution can then be analyzed for trends. Figure 9.8 illustrates the use of a histogram.

Figure 9.8

A histogram is a graphic representation of variations in a set of data.

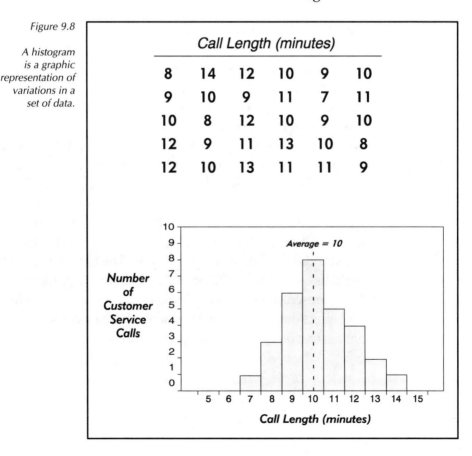

157

The average call length in our example is ten minutes. If the performance standard is nine minutes, there is a problem that must be addressed. We can either change the performance standard to be more realistic or evaluate why the calls are taking on average longer than expected. A cause-and-effect diagram is a useful tool for this analysis.

CHECK SHEETS

Check sheets are simple forms for recording data that have been designed to allow interpreting the results from the form itself. Using the example from the histogram in Figure 9.8, we may design a check sheet like the one shown in Figure 9.9. It could be used on a regular basis by the customer service representatives to monitor their personal performance relative to the call length established as the performance standard (in our example, it is nine minutes). When the check sheet reveals calls consistently exceeding the average, the representative can evaluate the cause immediately and take the appropriate corrective action. The service representative tracks calls that exceed the standard call length by call type. The excessive length for calls concerning billing and installation may mean that the representative needs training on these subjects. A cause and effect diagram can help to surface all the causes. Check sheets can be used for both PVI and PVR.

CHECK SHEET

Team Member: _Laura Reed_

Date: _January 21_

Shift: _2_

Place an "x" in the appropriate category when call length exceeds 9 minutes. Use space on bottom to note anything unusual.

	Billing	Delivery	Warranty	Installation
10				
9				
8	X			
7	X			
6	X			
5	X			
4	X			X
3	X			X
2	X	X		X
1	X	X	X	X

Notes: _New product shipped 1/20._
Short 2 people during shift.

RUN CHARTS

Run charts are simple line charts that can be used to identify trends. In the customer service example, we can chart total calls taken and average length of the call to see if performance is improving, holding steady, declining, or varying widely. The chart shows that on certain days of each week, specifically Monday and Friday, total call volume declines significantly while average call length increases. With this information, then we investigate the causes attributable to performance declines on these days. Run charts are useful for both PVI and for PVR. An example is shown in Figure 9.10.

Figure 9.10

Run charts are simple line charts that can be used to identify trends.

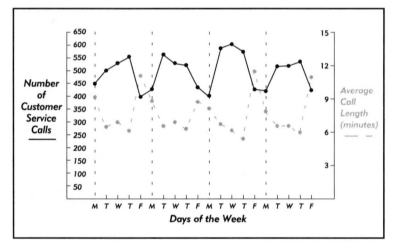

SCATTER DIAGRAMS

Scatter diagrams are a method of charting and analyzing the relationship between two variables. For example, the amount of employee training can be charted along with average length of customer service call per employee to see if there is a correlation. If there is a strong correlation, it does not necessarily mean that there is a cause-and-effect relationship. There could be other factors. For instance, anyone who has ever won the lottery also wears clothes, but that doesn't mean that one causes the other. If there is

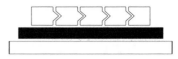

a correlation, further research can be conducted to determine if one factor is truly predictive of the other. Scatter diagrams can be used in both PVI and PVR efforts.

To create a scatter diagram, plot one of the variables along the x-axis, and the other along the y-axis. At the intersection, place a point. Do this for each of the pairs of values. If the two variables are correlated, the points will be arranged tightly around a line running diagonally from one corner of the graph to the other. An example is shown in Figure 9.11.

Figure 9.11

Scatter diagrams are a method of charting and analyzing the relationship between two variables.

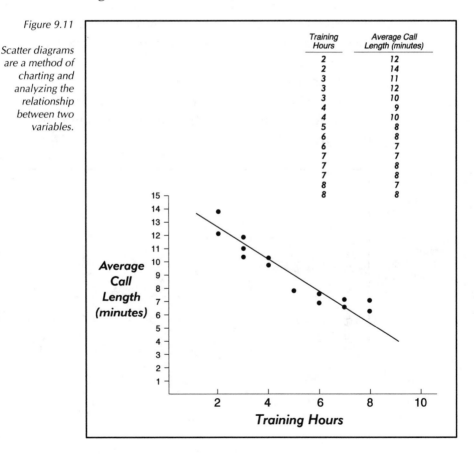

Training Hours	Average Call Length (minutes)
2	12
2	14
3	11
3	12
3	10
4	9
4	10
5	8
6	8
6	7
7	7
7	8
7	8
8	7
8	8

CONTROL CHARTS

Control charts are complex statistical tools. Here is an overview, but anyone serious about implementing control charts should reference detailed sources for additional information. Control charts operate on the premise that all processes have some inherent variance. Urgent attention should be paid to extreme variances from the average (called *special causes*), while normal variances (called *common causes*) should be ignored on a daily basis and improved through a long-term process improvement effort. Control charts are used primarily in manufacturing, but some companies have succeeded with them in other areas. Control charts are used almost exclusively in process value improvement, and rarely in PVR. There are several different kinds of control charts. One kind is shown in Figure 9.12.

Figure 9.12

Control charts are a tool for evaluating variations in processes that require special attention.

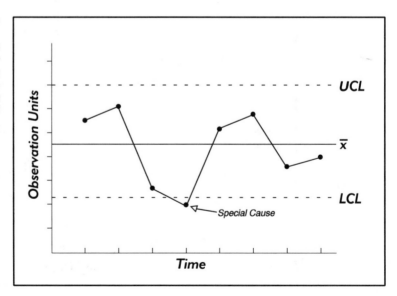

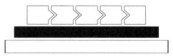

Data is accumulated, and then a statistical calculation of the Upper Control Limit (UCL), Lower Control Limit (LCL), and one other measure (data averages) are plotted on a graph. The individual data values are then plotted. Any special causes that exceed the UCL or LCL should be researched and addressed immediately. These special causes indicate that the process is "out of control." Over time, the process value improvement efforts should shrink the distance between the UCL and LCL. This would indicate an improvement in process stability.

PROCESS COST ANALYSIS

Traditional accounting methods produce ledgers and financial statements for departments and business units. How useful is this for companies that want to manage along processes? Where does a process owner turn to find out the total cost of their *process*? An accounting tool that is gaining acceptance in many companies today solves this problem and more. This new tool is called *Activity Based Costing* or *ABC* for short.

> None of us really understands what's going on with all these numbers.
> — David Stockman

Activity Based Costing is a more sophisticated version of its predecessor, cost accounting. It is more effective in associating costs with the activities that consume those costs because it breaks down overhead far more precisely. Advanced Micro Devices learned through ABC that certain products really cost 175% more to produce than they originally thought. This information led them to quickly begin altering product mix and adjusting product pricing.[1] ABC is an extensive and complex topic that won't be tackled here. However, there are many good reference books available about ABC.

A subset of ABC used in Total Process Management is called *process cost analysis (PCA)*. Process cost analysis is not nearly as accurate or as difficult to calculate as ABC, but it provides cost information suitable for improving process efficiency. With process cost analysis, the purpose is not to derive the cost of a product or customer as it is in ABC. The purpose of PCA is to determine the cost of *operations* in processes. The operation costs can be summarized to provide the cost of sub-processes, and then the cost of processes that they summarize to. Ultimately, you can determine the cost of the top-map processes. If your company has already implemented ABC, you know the cost of your processes and this exercise will be quite simple.

How is PCA information used? One use is to determine if you should outsource a process. Another use of the information is to drive improvements in process efficiency. Efficiency is a factor of cost and productivity. To improve efficiency you must reduce costs, increase productivity, or both. Developing a model of the process cost is essential to understanding and improving process efficiency. With processes, you can't just add up department costs because processes cut across departments.

Like activity-based costing, process cost analysis attributes costs to activities (operations) based on the factors that

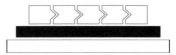

drive consumption of resources called *cost drivers*. In many cases, cost drivers may be units processed. There are many other possible cost drivers. Some of these may be batches processed, number of setups, sales dollars, average value of outstanding accounts receivable, and labor hours. Also, there may be several different cost drivers for a given operation. The important question to answer for each operation is *what causes the cost or consumption of resources?* These are the cost drivers.

Once the cost drivers are known, the cost information can be accumulated from traditional sources and associated with the operation. Summarizing the cost of all the operations gives the total process cost. Many people use process mapping software to store both the cost and the cost driver as data values in the operation itself. By storing the costs in the operations, the PVI workgroup or PVR project team can model the effect of alternative strategies for improving the processes and identify the best one. By the way, the effort required to calculate the process cost is one *very* good reason for having an accountant on your improvement team!

Consider the following example. RyCon Corporation (fictitious company) is performing a process reinvention project for the small order delivery process. RyCon has two kinds of orders:

- Bulk orders for the distribution channel and corporate resellers.

- Single orders of one to five units taken on a 1-800 line (called "small orders").

❖ Management is concerned about the profitability of the small order process and must decide whether to improve it or outsource it. None of the accounting reports provide the current cost per small order processed, so we must calculate it using process cost analysis. Three departments are involved in this process: inside sales, shipping, and accounts receivable. Only a portion of the costs from these departments is applicable to the small order process.

❖ Inside sales has two responsibilities: enter the small orders, and respond to customer service calls. Monthly departmental costs average $40,000 for ten people. Five people work on each of the two responsibilities. All the orders are for the small order process, but only 25% of the customer service calls are for small orders (there is no difference in call length between service calls for bulk vs. small orders). The cost driver in this case is *personnel*. The process cost from this department would be:

$40,000/10 people = $4,000 per person
Order taking cost:
5 people x $4000 = $20,000
Customer service cost:
(5 people) x 25% of the calls x $4,000 = $5000
Total process cost from this department:
$20,000 + $5000 = $25,000/month

❖ There are eight people in shipping, and the monthly departmental cost is $24,000 per month. Small orders contribute ten percent of the total number of units shipped. This would lead us to the conclusion that

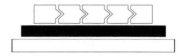

$2,400 (10% of the cost) belong to small orders. However, interviews reveal that the small orders take much longer to handle. As a result, the cost driver for shipping is *handling time*. Handling time for the small orders is 40% of the total. The real cost contribution is shown below.

$24,000/8 people = $3,000/person
Shipping cost:
(8 people) x 40% x $3,000 = $9,600/month

❖ Accounts Receivable has six people, and the monthly departmental cost is $15,000. The total revenue from small orders is 15% of the total. This would lead us to conclude that the prorated cost should be $2,250. However, it is harder to process the accounts receivable for small orders because the collection effort is more difficult. The cost driver in this case is *collection time*. The percent of collection time for small orders is 75% of the total. The cost contribution is shown below.

$15,000/6 people = $2,500/person
Accounts receivable cost:
(6 people) x 75% x $2,500 = $11,250/month

❖ Total monthly cost for the process is the sum of the allocation from the three departments.

Inside sales	$25,000
Shipping	$9,600
Accounts receivable	$11,250
Total/month	$45,850
Total/year	$550,200

❖ Revenue on small order sales is $600,000/year. When cost of goods sold and corporate overhead is added in, we learn that small orders are losing money. With this information, management determines that the PVR effort must reduce the process cost by at least 40%, or the process will be outsourced.

It is noteworthy that without process cost analysis, the allocation of costs to small orders would be understated by as much as $194,400/year ($86,400 from shipping and $108,000 from accounts receivable.) This could have led management to the erroneous conclusion that the small order process was profitable, and they may not have initiated corrective action.

CYCLE TIME ANALYSIS

Compared with process cost analysis, cycle time analysis is a breeze! Cycle time is the total time it takes to produce a unit of output from beginning to end in a process. Since the cycle time will vary based on exception processing and different kinds of transactions, it may be necessary to track several values. For instance, you may track average, minimum, and maximum cycle times. Your process improvement goal is to bring down all three cycle times.

Companies rarely track the time required for a transaction to travel the full length of the process. This is ironic given that cycle time is one of the areas in which companies can achieve *significant* competitive advantages.

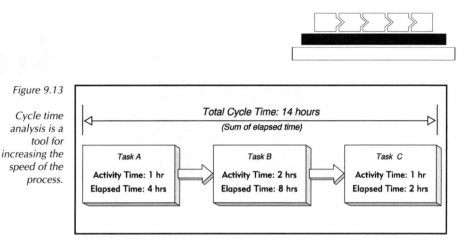

Cycle time is calculated by adding up the elapsed time for each operation in a process. The elapsed time is obtained through interviews discussed in Part 3, Evaluate the Current Environment, of the TPM methodology.

Much of the elapsed time in a process is in delays between operations where the work product sits and waits or is being transported from one place to another. As you might guess, eliminating delays between operations is a prime target for cycle time improvements. It can be difficult to get people to estimate the elapsed time, because many people simply do not know. In this situation, it may be necessary to track a few transactions through the process and record the times for yourself. This is also a good exercise for validating the elapsed time information from your interviews.

IMAGINE... 10
IT'S EASY IF
YOU TRY

Creative Brainstorming

_To know is nothing at all; to imagine is
everything._
— _Anatole France_

In the analytical, by-the-numbers, buttoned-down world
of modern business there is little encouragement of creativity and expression. What is the view in _your_ company
of people who do not follow the rules, who dare to be
different, or who challenge the status quo? Often they are
referred to as "wild ducks," non-conformists, trouble-
makers, and other names not repeatable here. Is it any
wonder that creativity and innovation are stifled in this
environment?

The world of business is the world of left-brain thinking.
The left side of our brain performs analytical thinking and
language. The right side of our brains is the source of creativity, imagination, and symbols. Many business activities require careful analysis and logical thought. When

riding in a car, we are glad that it has been engineered with analytical precision. The problem is that rational, logical thinking is the *only kind* of thinking allowed. Total Process Management can't be done with half a brain. It requires both left-brain analytical *and* right-brain creative thinking. After understanding the underlying causes of problems and process inefficiencies, the improvement teams need to brainstorm possible solutions. A summary of creative brainstorming techniques is provided in this chapter.

Analytical thinking is a major hindrance in creative brainstorming even though it is essential to effective business. Much of our problem-solving is ineffective because the only ideas allowed are those that can weather our left-brain analytical scrutiny. People suggesting ideas that don't meet the "reasonableness rule" are ridiculed or ignored. Most of the time when people get together to solve a problem, someone suggests a solution and immediately everyone debates its practical merits. Idea after idea is rejected until one idea survives the "gauntlet." Then the problem solving is over — one problem, one acceptable solution. People jump from the problem to the solution and rarely consider alternatives. This "ready-fire-aim" mentality must be overcome to generate creative, "out-of-the-box" thinking.

To illustrate this point, take a minute for the following exercise. Remove six letters from the list in Figure 10.1 so that the remaining letters (without changing their order) spell a familiar English word.[1] In our typical analytical fashion, most people jump to the conclusion that they are to remove a number of letters totaling six, rather than the

B S A I N X L E A T N T E A R S

actual letters themselves. If you didn't find the answer, try again. This time remove the following letters: "sixletters." The answer is at the end of this chapter.

Figure 10.2

Sometimes it takes a "whack on the side of the head" to break through our mental locks.

Roger von Oech, in his excellent book titled *A Whack on the Side of the Head*, describes ten mental locks to creativity.[2] Our challenge is to overcome these barriers and brainstorm the breadth of ideas necessary for true innovation. What does an effective brainstorming session look like? Well, there's just *one right way* to do them . . . NOT! The structure of a typical brainstorming session is shown on the following pages.

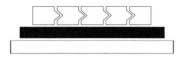

❖ *Establish a time for generating ideas* — usually 10 to 20 minutes. People will begin to analyze the ideas if it is longer than 30 minutes.

❖ *Write down ideas as people suggest them* — ask a volunteer to write where everyone can see.

❖ *Suggest ideas quickly* — encourage crazy ideas along with practical ones. People are more active and participative when standing.

❖ *Allow no questions or evaluation of any idea during this time* — no matter how crazy or stupid the ideas may sound.

❖ *Encourage everyone to contribute* — ask each person to provide an idea until the time is up. If the group is big enough, divide the group into two competitive teams — volume of ideas is the point here. You will always have a few really great ideas, and not always the ones expected. After all, it's creative brainstorming!

❖ *Shift from a creative mode to an analytical mode* — condense the ideas down into the top few using "piggybacking." This is where several ideas lead to similar but different ones. Through this technique a crazy idea can evolve into truly innovative one.

❖ *End up with no less than three valid ideas* — evaluate the pros and cons of each idea. A decision matrix is one tool for evaluating several alternatives. Figure 10.3 shows a sample decision matrix. Ultimately, one alternative will emerge as the top idea. Even if this was

Figure 10.3

A decision matrix
is a useful tool for
evaluating several
alternatives.

DECISION MATRIX	Cost	Savings	Risk Factor	Overall Rank
Solution #1	✔		✔	 👎
Solution #2	✔	✔	✔	 👍
Solution #3		✔		 👎

the idea everyone originally thought was the *one right solution*, the brainstorming effort was not wasted. The team can explain at least two other evaluated solutions and why they selected the one that they did.

Avoid the following pitfalls that limit the effectiveness of the creativity session.

❖ *Stick to the "one-rule" rule.* The only rule is to withhold judgment and/or analysis of ideas until the idea generation portion of the session is completed. This is hard. People want to ask what someone meant by an idea, immediately start analyzing an idea, or begin rejecting ideas. Be firm. Early analysis of ideas destroys the group's creativity.

❖ *Destroy your assumptions.* Everyone has their own "sacred cows"—those areas that are off limits to discussion. Start the session by having everyone list their assumptions and sacred cows. What is creativity if not challenging traditional thinking? When someone starts stakeholding, you can "moo" and point to the sacred cow list to remind them not to cling to old ways of thinking. (Just kidding about the "moo" part!)

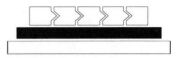

❖ *Deprive everyone of rank.* Participation and creativity are inhibited by rank. Ask everyone to write down his or her title on a piece of paper. Collect the papers in a box and set them outside the room. Announce that they can pick up their titles when they leave, but for the duration of the session everyone is equal.

(Answer to the SIXLETTERS riddle: Banana)

TOTAL PROCESS MANAGEMENT

PROCESS IMPROVEMENT CYCLE

EVALUATE THE CURRENT ENVIRONMENT • CONDUCT BENCH-MARKING • ESTABLISH CUSTOMER-DRIVEN STRETCH GOALS • BRAINSTORM INNOVATIONS • IMPLEMENT INNOVATIONS

TPM Part 3

Evaluate the Current Environment

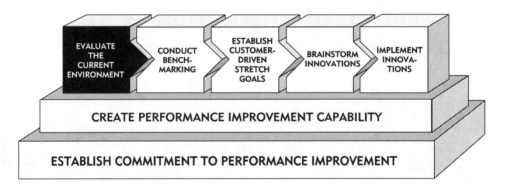

| EVALUATE THE CURRENT ENVIRONMENT | CONDUCT BENCH-MARKING | ESTABLISH CUSTOMER-DRIVEN STRETCH GOALS | BRAINSTORM INNOVATIONS | IMPLEMENT INNOVA-TIONS |

CREATE PERFORMANCE IMPROVEMENT CAPABILITY

ESTABLISH COMMITMENT TO PERFORMANCE IMPROVEMENT

STRANGERS IN A STRANGE LAND

11

Understanding Your Business

A man should know something of his own country, too, before he goes abroad.

—*Laurence Sterne*

Isn't it odd how we are strangers in our own companies? Most people can list their company's key products. They may even know the names of all of the corporate executives. But usually *no one* in the company can tell you the ten key corporate processes, so obviously they can't tell you how well those processes are operating either. Most employees cannot explain why they do the things they do in their jobs, or what the corporate mission statement is, or even what the other people in their department are doing. All of this information (and more) is essential if your company is serious about improving performance. Beginning with *Evaluate the Current Environment*, the last five parts of the Total Process Management methodology make up the *process improvement cycle*. The foundation section, TPM Parts 1 and 2, creates an environment in which sustained process improvement can occur. The process improvement cycle is the section of TPM in which the process improvements are made. This five-part cycle is repeated as frequently as there are improvement opportunities. The cycle is the same for process improvement and for process reinvention. The difference is in how the cycle is executed.

This part of the TPM methodology answers the question, *"What are we doing today?"* The following topics are discussed:

❖ Adapt the Process Improvement Cycle
❖ Identify and Prioritize Improvement Opportunities
❖ Conduct Interviews and Team Sessions
❖ Document and Evaluate Processes (Chapter 12)
❖ Document and Evaluate Systems (Chapter 13)
❖ Document and Evaluate Structure (Chapter 14)
❖ Document and Evaluate People (Chapter 15)

ADAPT THE PROCESS IMPROVEMENT CYCLE

Success with any methodology is predicated on adapting the methodology to your specific needs and circumstances. Total Process Management is designed for adaptability. It has seven *parts*, not *steps*. Steps imply an explicit order that must be followed. Like any other change management approach, TPM is most effective when imple-

Success with any methodology is predicated on adapting the methodology to your specific needs and circumstances.

mented in totality; however, it can and should be implemented in a number of combinations to meet individual needs. To repeat from earlier in the book: *Any performance improvement is worth having* even if it isn't as much improvement as might otherwise have been achieved.

To implement process value improvement (PVI), the process improvement cycle is executed by workgroups throughout the company, achieving incremental process improvements. Under PVI, a cycle may be completed in a few days, or in several months. Completion depends on the scope of the improvements and availability of resources.

For process value reinvention (PVR), an independent project team conducts the cycle one process at a time (usually a high-level process). The cycle has dramatic improvement objectives. Although the whole cycle can take a year to complete, the scale of improvements will be achieved quicker than comparable results through PVI. Companies should strive for a balance between process improvement implementation and process reinvention projects; except in rare circumstances, neither should be conducted to the exclusion of the other.

The process improvement cycle is shown in Figure 11.1. In this version, it is shown as a circle to indicate that the end of one cycle initiates another.

To illustrate one adaptation of the cycle, consider the following example. A major benchmarking effort is under-

Figure 11.1

In this version of
the process
improvement
cycle, the end of
one cycle initiates
another.

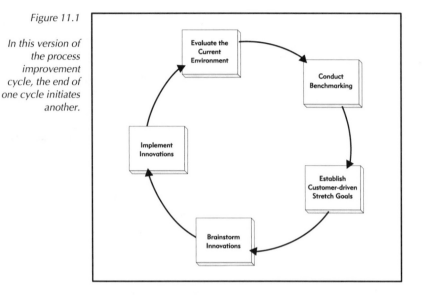

taken that provides information to support a number of process improvement efforts. Benchmarking need not be repeated for a while, but the remaining steps in the cycle will need to be repeated. In this case, the cycle may look like the one shown in Figure 11.2.

The number of variations is virtually endless. There are, however, several pitfalls that should be avoided.

❖ *Lack of knowledge about a company's own processes often leads to benchmarking failure.* It is essential that you understand your own environment before you begin to benchmark.

❖ *Benchmarked performance levels and best practices are quickly outdated.* A company should be careful to frequently renew the benchmark information. Otherwise,

you may find yourself chasing an outdated performance target. Even if you achieve it you could still be trailing the competition.

❖ *Companies can absorb only so much improvement project activity at any given time before reaching capacity.* Care should be taken not to overload an organization. Improvement projects could begin to overlap and conflict, the organization may not take time to institutionalize the improvements, and the improvement efforts may interfere excessively with ongoing operations. After all, the bills still have to be paid.

Figure 11.2

Here is a variation of the process improvement cycle. What variations would be needed for your company?

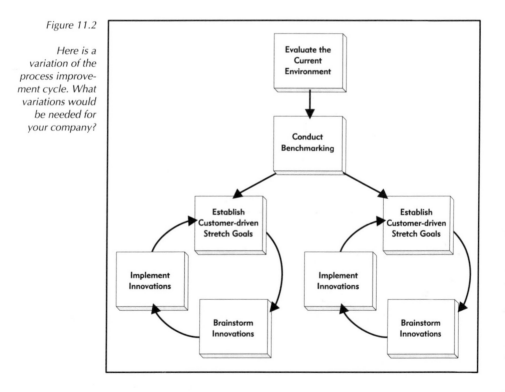

IDENTIFY AND PRIORITIZE
IMPROVEMENT OPPORTUNITIES

Whether you are conducting PVI or PVR improvements, the organization must select potential improvement opportunities from a number of alternatives. For process improvement, the process owner is responsible for coordinating the improvement efforts of process members and workgroups. In some circumstances, the process owner will set the PVI priorities. These decisions are coordinated with the TPM steering committee to ensure that there are no conflicts or overlaps with other efforts. The TPM steering committee is responsible for selecting and prioritizing key processes for PVR projects.

Each process improvement opportunity is ranked based on the potential impact on key criteria. Usually one of these is the impact on customer satisfaction. The other is the magnitude of the improvement opportunity; however, other criteria can be used instead. The improvement

Figure 11.3

Competing TPM opportunities can be evaluated and ranked based on key criteria.

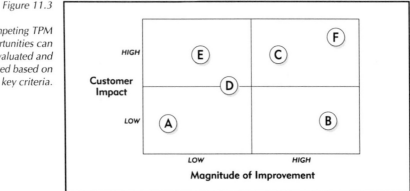

186

opportunities can then be plotted on a graph to help in prioritizing the candidates. In Figure 11.3, opportunities C and F are the top candidates for improvement. Other factors, such as readiness to change, competitive pressures, and strategic importance will influence which of these are selected. A Pareto chart and decision matrix are other tools that can be used to prioritize improvement opportunities (refer to Chapter 9).

CONDUCT INTERVIEWS AND TEAM SESSIONS

Information regarding the current processes, systems, structure, and people must be gathered from the organization. Two common methods are individual interviews and team design sessions. Both methods can be used for either PVI or PVR; however, interviews are used most commonly for process reinvention. Team design sessions are frequently used in both. The information gathered must be documented and evaluated for input into the brainstorming sessions discussed in Chapter 18. The following topics are discussed in this section of the chapter.

- ❖ Conduct Individual Interviews
- ❖ Conduct Team Design Sessions
- ❖ Document Business Issues
- ❖ Develop Analyses of the Data

Conduct Individual Interviews

Individual interviews are preferable when the information is highly sensitive and/or the process improvement team has sufficient time and resources. Also, confidential interviews result in more open and candid information. Process improvement interviews generally take two to four hours to conduct and an additional four to eight hours to document. There are several guidelines for interviewing.

❖ *Select an interview technique: structured, unstructured, or hybrid.* In structured interviews, the interviewers rigorously follow a prepared list of questions. In unstructured interviews, the interviewers provide loose guidelines and the interviewees share information in the order that they choose. The hybrid method combines the two methods.

There are advantages and disadvantages to each technique. Structured interviews require that the interviewer spend a significant amount of time preparing the questionnaire so that the necessary information is included. Since the interviewee is guided to answer specific questions, valuable information may not be obtained because the right question isn't asked.

In unstructured interviews, the interviewee is free to provide unsolicited information, but it may not be relevant to the interviewers. In the hybrid approach, develop a set of questions to ask but let the interviewees have some latitude to discuss things important to them. Many invaluable pieces of information are shared that would not have been asked. The prepared

list of questions ensures that you gather the necessary information.

❖ *Define the material to be gathered during the interview.* This can be either questions or a simple list, but should include information related to process, systems, structure, and people.

❖ *Determine whom to interview.* The interview list should include a cross-section of the organization, from top management to front-line workers. It should include someone knowledgeable for each part of the process. Customers and suppliers to the process should be interviewed as well. Always interview a secretary or administrative assistant. They know what is *really* going on in the organization. Try to interview only one person at a time, and never interview an employee and his or her boss at the same time. (How candid do you think the employee would be?) Several people can be interviewed at the same time if they all share the same function and are at the same reporting level in the organization.

> *Always interview the secretaries — they know what is really going on in an organization.*

The chief focus of TPM is improving value-added to the customer. Therefore, customers should be included in the interviews. Customers can also be people internal to the organization who use the work output from the operation or process. These internal customers can be called *clients* to avoid confusion with the true customers who purchase your products or services. Customers and clients should be asked to provide their requirements for the speed of service, cost (includes price and incidental factors), and quality of the goods and services provided. Customer surveys are excellent tools for obtaining information from a large population.

❖ *Establish the interview schedule.* Prepare and distribute notification of the time, place, purpose, and agenda to each of the people to be interviewed. If there is material that you want them to gather before the interview, let them know what it is (that is, reports, organization charts, process flowcharts). Try to conduct the interview in the interviewee's environment to put him or her at ease and to provide you with additional opportunity to observe environmental conditions.

❖ *Conduct the interviews in teams of two.* Usually one person will ask the questions and the second person will document the response. With only one person, much of the information is lost because it is difficult to lead an interview and write at the same time. Three or more people can be intimidating to the person being interviewed.

❖ *Set the stage at the start of the interview.* Explain to the interviewee that the information being gathered is confidential. The information may be shared with others, but it will not be attributed to any individual. Discuss the purpose of the interview, where you are in the process improvement process, and what happens next. Ask if there are any questions or concerns.

❖ *Control the interview.* It is very difficult to get people to answer your questions directly. People don't generally think about processes, so it is hard for them to talk about them. Also, everyone has a pet gripe and the interviewer is sure to hear about it. It is critical that the interviewer control the interview. Bring your rambling interviewee back to the topic at hand as gently as possible, but bring him back. Say something like, "That's very interesting information. We have limited time to gather a lot of information, so we need to get back to the question . . ."

People may be reluctant to talk with you due to fear, suspicion, or hostility. It is important to draw these people out. Try getting them to talk about their favorite subject, even if it is irrelevant, and then guide them back to your questions.

Ask open questions that require the interviewee to respond in their own words. Avoid "yes" or "no" questions or ones that lead the interviewee to a particular response.

❖ *Review and summarize the material immediately.* This is important to ensure that the key information is captured while it is still fresh, and to obtain consensus among the interview team about the information gathered. Ask the interviewee to review the material and provide corrections and clarifications.

> *The biggest mistake in estimating time requirements is in how long it takes to document the material gathered in interviews.*

If at all possible, this information should be recapped with the interviewee prior to leaving the interview. In my experience, the biggest mistake in estimating time requirements is in how long it takes to document the material gathered in interviews. As a rule of thumb, for each hour of interview, allow at least two hours for documentation and analysis.

Summary: Conduct Individual Interviews

- Select an interview technique: structured, unstructured, or hybrid.
- Define the material to be gathered during the interview.
- Determine whom to interview.
- Establish the interview schedule.
- Conduct the interviews in teams of two.
- Set the stage at the start of the interview.
- Control the interview.
- Review and summarize the material immediately.

Conduct Team Design Sessions

In team design sessions, representatives from each part of the process meet in a large room to brainstorm the process improvement opportunity. For process value improvement, this usually is a problem-solving session in which the causes of a problem may need to be brainstormed. Process reinvention projects use these sessions to gather a lot of information quickly, similar to the

Joint Application Design (JAD) sessions frequently used in information system design. Interviews may take several months, but team design sessions can be completed in a few hours (PVI) or days (PVR). These team design sessions are a better choice when there is limited time or resources, and when candor is not required. Some guidelines for team design sessions are discussed below.

❖ *Select the appropriate people for the session.* The participants should include a cross-section of people from top to bottom and across all of the functions that participate in the process. Customers and clients and suppliers should participate if at all possible.

❖ *Try to limit the group to 15 or less.* When there are more than 15 people, it becomes difficult to remain focused. Also, some people may not participate when there are too many people involved.

❖ *Set the stage at the start.* Begin the session by agreeing to a problem statement or common understanding of the purpose. Communicate the reason that each person has been invited to attend, and what his or her contribution is expected to be. Agree to the work products to be generated by the group.

❖ *Keep the group focused.* People will want to talk about any number of subjects unrelated to the topic at hand. For this reason, it is essential that the group have an independent moderator.

❖ *Document and post the work products as you go.* This lets the team keep track of the progress being made (or lack thereof). After the session, submit a draft of the work products to the participants for review and acceptance.

Summary: Conduct Team Design Sessions

- Select the appropriate people for the session.
- Try to limit the group to fifteen or less.
- Set the stage at the start.
- Keep the group focused.
- Document and post the work products as you go.

Document Business Issues

Business issues are problems identified within the current process that are barriers to improvement, causes of inefficiencies, rules with no purpose, quality failures, lack of information, and any other condition that reduces performance. Business issues are identified and documented during the interviewing process.

It is important with business issues that you capture a statement of the business practice or problem, and why it is a problem. Possible solutions can be documented but aren't required. Business issues are used in TPM Part 6, Brainstorm Innovations, as ideas about how the current process needs to be improved. Look at a sample business issue in Figure 11.4

Figure 11.4

Business issues
are problems
identified within
the current
process that
reduce perfor-
mance.

Business Issue

Business practice: A second approval is required for any purchase over $50.

Business Impact: Almost every purchase is over $50 which means that management must approve an excessive amount of documents. This causes delays, excessive administration in tracking the approval, and is inefficient for management because the risk is insignificant based on total dollar exposure.

Possible solutions: Eliminate most second approvals. Raise the dollar value for purchases requiring second approval.

Develop Analyses of the Data

Information gathered in the interviews and group design sessions supports activities throughout the remainder of the process improvement cycle. Prior to completion of this part of the cycle, it is important for the process improvement team to use some of the problem-solving and analysis tools to evaluate the information. These analyses will serve as input into the remaining parts of the cycle. All of the problem-solving and analysis tools discussed in Chapter 9 can be applied to the information gathered in interviews.

❖ *Process maps* are a requirement for process improvement.

❖ *Cause-and-effect diagrams* can be used to identify the causes of problems.

❖ *Pareto charts* will help identify and rank the top causes of problems.

❖ *Histograms* can identify trends in process variations.

❖ *Run charts* can show trends in process performance.

❖ *Scatter diagrams* can identify correlations between data and identify problem causes.

❖ *Control charts* can reveal problem areas and signal whether improvement efforts are reducing process variances.

❖ *Process cost analysis* is important for determining cost measures.

❖ *Cycle time analysis* is essential for determining the speed in which the process is conducted.

The analytical tools can be applied to any information gathered in the interviews. It is essential that *each business issue* be analyzed prior to the brainstorming session discussed in Part 6 of TPM.

GO WITH THE FLOW(CHART)

12

Document and Evaluate Processes

*"Journey over all the universe
in a map . . . "*
— *Cervantes*

The first of the four organizational levers of change, *process*, is discussed in this chapter. The intent is on capturing information about the flow of activities that deliver value to our customers.

DEVELOP PROCESS MAPS

The fundamental tool for understanding and evaluating processes for improvement opportunities is the process map. As defined in Chapter 9, process maps are a form of flowchart that capture substantially more information than a standard process diagram. In addition to the information included in a flowchart, process maps include

Figure 12.1

Operations and
process maps can
include the
information
shown here.

Any shape on the process map where action is taken is called an *operation*. Some or all of the following information can be captured for each operation:

- Responsibility for performing the operation — Usually the job title.

- Operation description — Brief description of the action taken.

- Cost/Resources consumed — Cost per unit, number of hours, or full-time equivalent people required for the task over a fixed time period.

- Activity time — Time required to actually perform the task.

- Elapsed time — Entire time a unit is being processed including wait time (often called lag time).

- Volume measures — Units or transactions processed (remember to identify the transaction type).

- Activity mode — On-line, batch, or manual.

- Performance measures — Measures for current performance expectations.

- Frequency — How often the activity is performed.

- Value-added classification — Whether the operation adds value for the customer or not.

certain characteristics that further define the process. These were discussed in detail in Chapter 9. For your convenience, they are reproduced in Figure 12.1.

DOCUMENT PROCESSING RULES

In addition to the information listed above, it is important to document the processing rules, and to be alert to unusual operations or obvious inefficiencies. It is appropriate (and necessary) to ask the reason that these operations are performed and rules are needed. Avoid the word "why" because it is both challenging and accusatory. Try a statement like, "Can you help me understand the purpose of that action?" More often than not, the answer will be "we've always done it that way." These are candidates for business issues.

ASSESS PROCESS PERFORMANCE

For process improvement, there are three measures (also called *metrics*) that are critical.

1) Speed (cycle time)
2) Cost (efficiency)
3) Quality (effectiveness)

Some sources advocate customer satisfaction as a separate measure. However, since customer satisfaction is a reflection of performance in speed, cost, and quality, the focus will be only on these three. These metrics usually can be captured at an operation level; although, quality may be best measured at an overall process level.

Speed is determined by the *elapsed time* for operations in the process. Speed (also called cycle time) for each operation should be documented in the interview or team design session. This information is often unreliable so the improvement team should independently validate the cycle time. This can be achieved by tracking several transactions through the process and documenting the times at each point in the process map. This is also a good way to validate the accuracy of the process map.

Cost (efficiency) is the combination of labor, direct cost, and indirect cost consumed for the operation to produce a given amount of output. This information is essential for building consensus that the cost of certain tasks is not worth the value delivered. Process cost analysis, discussed at length in Chapter 9, is the primary tool for developing cost information. The second element of efficiency is the amount of output from the process. Efficiency can be improved by increasing output at the same cost, decreasing cost for the same output, or both. As a result, the improvement team should document the type and amount of output created for each operation.

Quality is determined by how well the process produces goods and services that meet or exceed customer requirements. Quality can be measured internally through the number of customer service calls, number of product returns, percentage of defective products, and other such indicators. In addition to the internal measures of quality

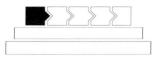

mentioned above, we need to devise and execute a mechanism that allows customers to *directly* rate their perception of the quality of our processes. These can be in the form of interviews, questionnaires, or surveys.

DEVELOP THE VALUE-ADDED RATIO

One of the characteristics captured for operations in the process map is the value-added classification. Each operation is assessed to determine if it adds value from the customer's perspective. The rule of thumb is simple — if the customer will pay you to do it, then it is value-added, otherwise, it is non-value-added. Almost everything in a process is non-value-added. For instance, mailing, transporting, inspecting, approving, reworking, preparing, filing, copying, and wait time are all non-value-added. These are the targets for improving the process. You may still need to do many of these things in order for the process to work, but our goal is to eliminate as many as possible. The tools for eliminating the non-value-added activities are the process improvement principles discussed in Chapter 8.

Almost everything in a process is non-value-added.

Some people advocate two value-added categories. The first is *customer* value-added and the second is *business* value-added. Business value-added activities are those that are in the interests of the company, but the customer doesn't value them. Some examples are government regulations, various professional standards (such as accounting), and internal rule-making bodies (internal audit). I don't recommend tracking business value-added activities because it is too easy to attach this classification to sacred cows that should be eliminated. For instance, management approvals could be considered business value-added even though they are a prime target for process improvement. One approach is to recognize that some activities are required by regulatory bodies and leave them classified as non-value-added to the customer. (Maybe you will want to lobby for those non-value-added regulations to be changed — many companies have done it!)

A *value-added ratio* can be calculated to illustrate the importance of the need to change. This is done by summing the cycle time for the value-added activities and dividing it by the total cycle time. The resulting value is usually less than five percent. In most cases this is a startling piece of information, both to management and to the process participants. The ratio can be presented graphically, usually as a pie chart.

Summary: Document and Evaluate Processes

- Develop process maps.
- Document processing rules.
- Assess process performance:
   - Speed
   - Cost
   - Quality
- Develop value-added ratio.

AVOIDING THE COWPATH

13

Document and Evaluate Systems

"Our little systems have their day."

— *Tennyson*

The second of the four organizational levers of change is *systems*. Information technology is one of the key enablers of process change. The process improvement team must identify the information systems used in the current environment as well as the user's evaluation of the effectiveness of those systems. Many of our information systems have been developed to emulate the way the business was being conducted at the time. The systems did not improve the processes in any measurable way. They simply did the same old inefficient and non-value-added activities faster. This is analogous to putting a super highway where the cows have always walked — we have just been *paving the cowpath*. The process improvement team is responsible for identifying where this has occurred and developing recommendations for improving the information systems to support world-class processes.

In addition to software systems, it is important to evaluate the availability of key office machinery. This includes computer terminals, personal computers, printers, copiers, fax machines, and telephones. Last, the process improvement team should assess the use of the latest technologies. Any problems or deficiencies can be documented as business issues.

Document the Software Systems

The software systems being used in the current process can be identified in a number of ways. The most obvious way is to ask people what systems they are using. However, surprisingly few users can tell you what systems they use — they know how to use them, but not what they are. This leads to our second source — the management information systems (MIS) department. Most MIS departments maintain an inventory of the systems that they have and who uses them. Their circumstance is often opposite that of the system users — they know what the systems are, but not how they are used.

Evaluate User Satisfaction with Software Systems

Getting an understanding of whether or not the systems meet the users' needs, and the degree of inefficiency (if any) being experienced is more difficult than the previous part. This evaluation is not intended to be a "requirements definition" exercise, which is extremely time-con-

suming. At this point, we want to define the problem, not the solution. This information can be obtained through the interview process with some well-placed questions. It is helpful for users to show the interviewers examples of how the system is inefficient.

Evaluate the Availability of Key Office Equipment

One of the major sources of inefficiencies in office environments is access to key office equipment. Sometimes people sit idle for long periods of time because they have to share a computer terminal that is in use. Everyone has had the experience of walking all the way across a building to access a fax machine or printer. This is true even for jobs that require constant interaction with these machines! The loss in productivity during this downtime is significant and should be addressed by the process improvement team.

There are three pieces of information that should be captured regarding the office equipment. They are type, suitability for its use, and physical location. The example in Figure 13.1 shows one way to document the availability of office machines. The suitability for use can be included as another column, or can be noted separately.

One of the things this type of analysis can reveal is disproportionate allocation of equipment between workgroups. In one company, several secretaries had the most powerful personal computers on the market but computer programmers were working with machines that were two and three generations old!

Figure 13.1

An office machine inventory is useful for evaluating hardware needs and inefficient or inequitable allocation of hardware.

Type	Mgmt	Admin	Dev	Quality Assurance
Personal Computers				
486/66 DX Tower	1	4	4	2
486/33 SX Tower	2		10	2
486/50 portables	5		4	
386/33 Tower			5	6
IBM AT			2	
Printers				
HP Laserjet 3P	8	4		
HP Laserjet 35i	1		2	1
FAX				
Mita CDC 550	2	2	1	1
PanaFax UF-250		2		
Number of People	8	4	25	10

The physical location of office equipment is best documented through a floor plan. The floor plan can be modified to show typical traffic patterns to and from the equipment. This particular piece of analysis can be developed in conjunction with the "structure" organizational lever for change (discussed in the next chapter).

Document Use of the Latest Technologies

The process improvement team should be alert to opportunities to leverage the latest technologies. Consider the example below:

One company, whose benefits administration process I was helping with, provided a tour of their document storage facility. This company kept tens of thousands of folders—one for each current and past employee. They were quite proud of their state-of-the-art document storage equipment; however, I noticed that employees were constantly getting up and going to the files to access the information there. As it turns out, this was an area that could have used electronic document imaging to eliminate on-site document storage and drastically streamline their research efforts.

There is *always* some technology that could be used to improve a process—some significantly, others incrementally. The ability to recognize these opportunities is predicated on previous knowledge of what technologies are available. This is a strong reason for having an MIS department representative on the improvement team, or for using a knowledgeable consultant. Benchmarking is another source for identifying enabling technologies.

Summary: Document and Evaluate Systems

- Document the software systems.
- Evaluate user satisfaction with software systems.
- Evaluate the availability of key office equipment.
- Document use of the latest technologies.

LAYERS ARE FOR CAKES, NOT COMPANIES

14

Document and Evaluate Structure

"In a hierarchy, every employee tends to rise to his level of incompetence."
— *Laurence Johnston Peter*

Cakes should have a lot of layers, not companies! The third organizational lever for change is structure. Here we consider not only the traditional organization structure, but also the structure of the physical work environment.

DOCUMENT THE PHYSICAL LAYOUT

Poorly conceived physical work environments can be significant barriers to organizational effectiveness and efficiency. Closely related workgroups are often separated geographically. Office machines are in distant or inconvenient locations. Offices may be too big, too small, or

poorly laid out for office traffic. Each of these represent business issues that can lead to process improvements.

Create a Campus Map

The physical work environment should be documented graphically to illustrate the inefficiencies inherent in poor office layouts. One graphic should show the office buildings and connections among groups aligned along a single process. This is called a campus map even though the buildings may be in different cities, or even different countries. An example is shown in Figure 14.1.

Poorly conceived physical work environments can be significant barriers to organizational effectiveness and efficiency.

Figure 14.1

A campus map is used to illustrate inefficient organization of workers across separate buildings.

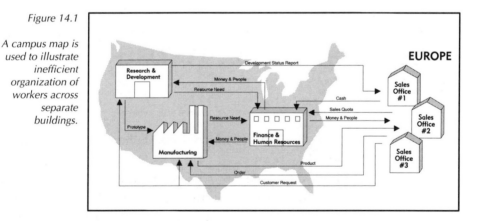

Create Building Floor Plans

Another graphic can be the floor plan of an individual building. The floor plan can show the connections between groups within the same building who are aligned along a

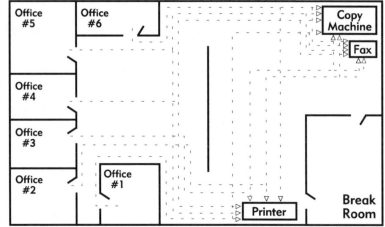

Figure 14.2

A floor plan can show inefficiencies in organization of workers within a single building.

single process. They can also show the location of and traffic pattern to key office equipment. A sample floor plan of the latter is shown in Figure 14.2.

DOCUMENT THE MANAGEMENT HIERARCHY

How are companies like onions? When you peel back the layers, they both make you cry. The organizational hierarchy is an important tool for evaluating the organization's managerial style and operating effectiveness. It is important not to confuse formal organization charts with the way that the organization really works.

Document the Formal Hierarchy

Copies of published organization charts should be obtained for reference purposes. However, the process improvement team should also construct a diagram of the management hierarchy from information obtained in the interviews. Formal organization charts are frequently outdated and so cannot be relied upon. Also, they often omit temporary and contract employees that add to headcount. This "true" headcount can be used as a gauge of productivity through ratios such as revenue/headcount, transactions processed/headcount, and cost/headcount.

Document the Informal Hierarchy

There are usually one or more undocumented informal layers of management that should be identified and documented. These informal layers add to the organizational bureaucracy and are strong candidates for elimination. The informal management positions can only be revealed through the interview process and from direct observation — job titles and formal organization charts are unreliable sources. Here is a tip — ask the front-line workers (or secretaries) about the management structure. They will usually know and be glad to tell you.

Other indications of line positions that are really management positions are references to "work leadership," "team leaders" (they are rarely true facilitators), "senior" positions of any sort, positions that have "assistants," and people with responsibilities for review and approval of the work products of co-workers.

Analyze the Management Span of Control

Once the true organizational hierarchy is established, calculate the average span of control. Count the number of
people managing other employees and divide that number into the total number of employees. The higher the
final number is, the flatter the organization is and the less
bureaucracy exists. For most organizations, this number
is below ten. For world-class companies, it ranges from
15 – 30! Highly technical groups will generally have a lower span of control than will administrative groups. For
instance, engineers may have a span of control of six to
eight, while order processing may have a span of 25. If
the span of control is too narrow, develop a business issue. A sample analysis is shown in Figure 14.3.

Figure 14.3

*Span of control
and organiza-
tional levels
analysis can
reveal excessive
management.*

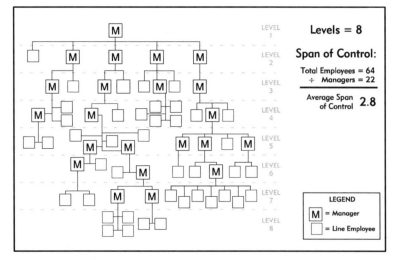

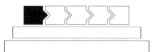

Analyze the Number of Organizational Levels

The number of levels in the organization, measured from the top officer for the business unit to the front-line worker, is another indication of corporate bureaucracy. Numbers of five or less indicate relatively flat organizations. Anything over five suggests room for improvement. Flat organizations are an absolute requirement for worker empowerment — excessive management layers get in the way of the real work with unnecessary rules and bureaucracy. Once again, if there are too many organizational levels, develop a business issue.

Summary: Document and Evaluate Structure

◆ Document the physical layout.

- Create a campus map.
- Chart building floor plans.

◆ Document the management hierarchy.

- Document the formal hierarchy.
- Document the informal hierarchy.
- Analyze the management span of control.
- Analyze the number of organizational levels.

AIN'T WE GOT CULTURE? 15

"The only way we beat the competition is with people. That's the only thing anybody has. Your culture and how you motivate and empower and educate your people is what makes the difference."[1]
— *Robert Eaton, CEO, Chrysler*

The fourth organizational lever for change is *people*. "People" or *culture* is the *single strongest influence* on the success or failure of implementing change. It is also the most overlooked. The best business practices in the world are worth nothing if the employees do not implement them. It is essential that the process improvement team accurately assess the people dimension of change and identify opportunities for improvement. This chapter discusses the following topics:

- ❖ Mission and Strategy
- ❖ Corporate Values
- ❖ Change Readiness

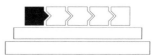

- ❖ Communication Systems
- ❖ Measurement and Reward Systems
- ❖ Employee Skills

MISSION AND STRATEGY

The corporate mission and strategy provide the unifying elements for business operations. Each department (and ultimately each process) should have a mission that ties it to the overall corporate direction. If this does not exist or is inconsistent with the corporate mission, the organization may be operating at cross-purposes. The goal for the improvement team is to document any discrepancies between the departmental missions and strategies and the corporate mission and strategy. There are several steps required to do this.

- ❖ *Identify the departmental missions and strategies.* Start by asking to understand the missions and strategies of the departments involved in the process. In some cases this is already documented, but in most it is not. When it isn't, try to construct the implicit mission using input from several departmental members. (Their statements of the mission will almost always be different.)

- ❖ *Identify how well the corporate mission and strategy is understood.* One of the indicators of mission congruence is how well employees understand the corporate mission and relate it to their job. If they don't understand the mission, then it is likely that their actions and decisions are not consistent with the corporate direction.

❖ *Compare the departmental and corporate missions and strategies.* If there is any inconsistency between departmental and corporate missions and strategies, then there may be opportunities to improve performance by bringing the department's activities back in line with the corporate mission. These should be documented as business issues.

CORPORATE VALUES

Corporate values shape employee decisions at every level, so it is essential that the values support world-class operations. In many companies, these values are published. However, the true values can be identified only through observation of employee behavior, communications, and decision making. Once the true corporate values are known, the team must determine if the values support the behavior that leads to world-class operations. Typical values include risk taking versus avoidance, individualism versus teamwork, revenue generation versus profitability, and internal political focus versus external customer focus.

❖ *Assess the formal corporate values.* Almost every company has developed and published the desired corporate values. The process improvement team should determine through the interviews how well the for-

mal corporate values are understood. If there is a poor understanding, then this can be documented as a business issue.

❖ *Identify the informal corporate values.* There is a big difference between the published corporate values and what they *really* are. It is essential to understand these informal values, because they form the hidden barriers to process improvement efforts. Earlier in the book the example of American Vice-President Al Gore's efforts to reinvent the American government was used. You will not find a government cultural value published anywhere that says "avoid risk." However, that does not mean that this value is not a real and very powerful force in defeating efforts at innovation and change in government.

The informal values must be identified through research and direct observation. Some of the sources that can reveal informal corporate values are listed below.

- Formal policies and procedures
- Internal memos and electronic communications
- Organization structure
- Management practices
- Degree of cooperation
- Quality of work life
- Employee motivation and morale
- Degree of innovation and corporate change

- Company and departmental meetings
- Company newsletters
- Employee turnover
- Degree of "caste system" stratification
- Degree of office gossip and innuendo
- Employee performance appraisal and compensation

❖ *Assess informal corporate values.* Once the informal corporate values are understood, they should be evaluated to determine if they support the behavior desired by the corporate leadership. If not, this should be documented as a business issue.

CHANGE READINESS

An organization's readiness for change is a function of commitment (will) and ability (skill) to change. Total Process Management Parts 1 and 2 comprise the foundation section of the methodology, which is designed to address these two concerns. However, here is where the current status of the organization's skill and will to change is *evaluated*. If the people aren't willing or able to change, then efforts to implement change are going to fall far short of expectations.

If the people ain't ready, the bus ain't leavin'!

The organizational skill and will to change must be evaluated at each level of the organization (for example, exec-

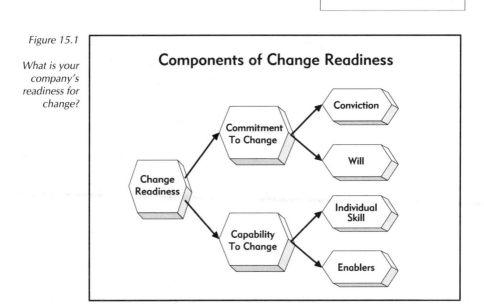

Figure 15.1

What is your company's readiness for change?

Components of Change Readiness

Change Readiness

Commitment To Change

Conviction

Will

Capability To Change

Individual Skill

Enablers

utives, middle managers, front-line supervisors, staff). This assessment will identify corrective measures necessary to ensure that the process improvements are accepted, implemented, and continually improved. A sample change readiness assessment is shown in Figure 15.2.

❖ *Assess Commitment to Change.* The two components that contribute to commitment to change are conviction and will. *Conviction* is the intellectual understanding of the need to change. *Will* is the emotional response to the need for change. Keys to solving problems in these areas are communication of the change drivers and employee involvement in the change process. These topics were discussed at length in Chapter 6.

An important tool in understanding the will to change is *stakeholder analysis.* Using this technique, the process improvement team identifies key people or positions who have the most "at stake" in the change process (i.e., power, responsibility, "turf"). These stakeholders are characterized as *enthusiasts*, *followers*, or *opponents*. They are mapped to the degree of change to be experienced. This tool enables the team to focus effort on the people needing the most attention. A sample stakeholder analysis is shown in Figure 15.3.

> *You're either part of the solution or part of the problem.*
> — *Eldridge Cleaver*

♦ *Enthusiasts* are people who actively support the proposed change. In some circumstances, their enthusiasm must be "reined in" to prevent antagonizing fellow employees.

♦ *Followers* are people who will do just what they are told and no more. They will not hurt the change process, but they are not likely to help it either.

♦ *Opponents* are people who are dead set against the proposed change. They will actively oppose the project, build supporting coalitions, and exercise as much political clout as they can wield. Some even resort to sabotage. Ironically, these people can become the greatest supporters for the change if they can be "won over" to the new point of view. One key to successful implementation of change is to enlist these people into the improvement

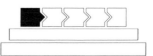

Figure 15.2

A Change Readiness Assessment can help to evaluate the current status of an organization's skill and will to change. How ready is your organization for change?

CHANGE READINESS ASSESSMENT				
Project: PVR - New Product Delivery			By: _MDY_ Date: _1/20_	
	Committment		Capability	
Job Class/Person	Conviction	Will	Individual Skill	Enablers
Executive Management	Clear understanding of the need to change. Undecided on how to do it.	Unwilling to take a strong stand—worried about losing old cultural values. Concerned about costs required for change.	Can lead the change process but don't know how. Don't have empowering team skills.	Unable to fund large systems projects. Middle management can stonewall changes.
Middle Management	Low: most were promoted from within. Little experience with other ways of doing things.	Opposed to changes that will threaten their jobs and their power positions.	Weak: core skills have not been maintained. Do not understand teamwork. Poor problem-solving skills.	Poor: no training systems are available. Strong com- and and control culture. Performance measures and incentives support low risk and status quo.
Front-Line Employees	See the need to change. Unsure about how it will be possible with the current management.	Concerned that this will turn into an excuse for across-the-board layoffs.	More advanced in PC literacy. Open to learning new skills, feel held back by entrenched power-players in middle management.	Lack access to sufficient personal computing. Centralized systems are inflexible, expensive and unresponsive. Command and control management style stifles innovation.

Figure 15.3

Stakeholder analysis can reveal the people with the most to gain or lose from the changes. Who are the stakeholders for your business processes?

STAKEHOLDER ANALYSIS			
Project: PVR - New Product Delivery			By: _MDY_ Date: _1/20_
Department	Job Class/Person	Type	Comments
CEO	Ryan Griffith	E	Change is required for customer focus
Marketing and Sales	Management Marketing professionals Salespersons	E E F	Perceived as receiving much more influence as a result of the change
Development	Management:		
	George Smith	O	Perceives loss of power
	Sally Lee	O	Perceives loss of power
	Gordon Sellers	F	Will support Sally
	Rae Swisher	E	New to company: sees no need to change
	Development Managers	O	Perceive loss of esteem
	Engineers	E	Relieved to have clear expectations

Type: E = Enthusiast   F = Follower   O = Opponent

221

team   and make them part of the solution.

❖ *Assess Ability to Change.* Ability is comprised of the two elements, individual skill and enablers. *Individual skill* is a measure of the education and training required for an employee to operate in the new environment. *Enablers* are the systems and technology that facilitate operating in the reengineered environment. Each must be assessed in order to understand the investments in employee education and technology required for the proposed changes.

COMMUNICATION SYSTEMS

A distinction is made here between the manner in which information travels through an organization (the human communication system) and the hardware that supports communication. Here we are emphasizing the human communication systems. Key information is spread through organizations using both formal and informal communication systems.

Poor communication is one of the key reasons that organizational change fails.

❖ *Assess the formal communication systems.* Formal systems include memos, electronic mail, videos, and various types of meetings. Much of the success of Total Process Management is predicated on effective communication between the change leadership and the rest of the organization. I cannot say this strongly

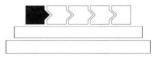

enough: poor communication is a primary reason that organizational change fails.

If the formal communication systems are ineffective, employees will use informal systems. This leads to loss of productivity and the even more serious result of miscommunication. In the words of one consultant, "People abhor information vacuums; when there is no on-going conversation as part of the change process, gossip fills the vacuum. Usually the rumors are much worse and more negative than anything that is actually going on."[2]

In Chapter 6, several ways to communicate during the change process are discussed in detail. During this part of TPM, we are intent on assessing the effectiveness of formal communications. Is there a communication plan? If there isn't one, then that is a business issue that should be addressed immediately. If there is one, the improvement team should assess its effectiveness. Are the steps in the plan being completed as planned? Is there broad-based awareness of the message that is being communicated? Have people related the message to themselves and internalized it? Do the employees feel that their concerns have been listened to and validated? Many of these questions can be answered through the interview process. If there are deficiencies, document them as business issues and address them to the change leadership immediately.

Informal channels of communication result when the formal communication systems are ineffective.

❖ *Assess informal communication systems.* Informal systems are characterized by gossip, innuendo, and rumors. (Sound familiar?) These informal channels result in organizational inefficiency and lack of focus. Informal channels of communication result when the formal communication systems are ineffective. People will find out what is happening one way or another. When they can't find out through the formal mechanisms, they go around them.

Some informal communication is unavoidable and provides a healthy emotional outlet for employees. However, it can get out of hand quickly and become a real concern for the change team. The informal channels of communication can be assessed through observation and asking specific questions during interviews. The improvement team can take note of hallway and break room conversations about the change process, and the general employee attitudes being aired. Comments like "management is only out for themselves," "this is just another fire drill — it too will pass," and "this is just a move by so-and-so to save his job (or grab power)" are indications that the formal channels aren't working.

The team can also ask employees in the interviews what they know about the change process, and why the company is doing it. Ask them where they learned of these things. If any of the answers are cause for concern, note them as business issues and alert the change leadership. Communication problems cannot wait — they must be addressed immediately.

MEASUREMENT AND REWARD SYSTEMS

What gets measured gets done. Surprisingly few organizations measure performance consistently and effectively. Usually, we make the mistake of measuring activity rather than results (for example, sales calls rather than sales generated). Information should be gathered about how performance is measured for the department, individual job classes, and for the process (if it is measured at all). In addition, the improvement team should identify and evaluate how performance is rewarded.

❖ *Assess performance measures.* This information is needed for each department participating in the process. It may be formally documented or only available from the management of those areas. Through the interviews, determine if the employees are aware of the performance measures. Look to see if the measures are posted publicly and if performance for the group and individuals is tracked over time. Are the measures consistent with the overall outcome *for the process*, or do they optimize department outcomes? Any problems should be documented as business issues.

Organizations should measure things that can be used to improve the process speed, cost, or quality. The data captured should also support the reward system. However, many companies make the mistake of only tracking measures related to rewards. Many activities should be measured that can help with analysis and problem solving, but are not an appropriate basis for compensation incentives. An example of something that you should measure, but not reward, is average call length for customer service reps. This can be used for diagnostics, but isn't an appropriate reward. Customer satisfaction and answering 100% of incoming calls are more appropriate for rewards.

❖ *Assess performance rewards.* Compensation and performance rewards are powerful motivators (although not the only motivator). Rewards generally are the same for groups of job classes. Many of the same questions from above are relevant here. Are employees aware of how they are rewarded? Are the rewards applied consistently? Do the rewards support the corporate values and mission of the company? Are we measuring factors that support the rewards? Do the rewards encourage behavior that will optimize the process? Once again, problems should be documented as business issues.

A key mistake that companies make in establishing compensation incentives is to reward activity, and not results. This encourages lots of activity (churning of work) and not the bottom-line results.

In one example, I worked with a company to improve the order fulfillment process. The group rewarded each sales person on *number of calls* taken. That is an activity. We changed the reward system and based it on revenue generated *and* customer satisfaction rating (obtained through weekly surveys). This resulted in increased sales *and* the number of calls taken stayed high because that is a key element of customer satisfaction.

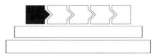

EMPLOYEE SKILLS

Total Process Management results in changes to jobs and responsibilities. Employees must have the skills required to adapt to these changing job requirements. The process improvement team must gain an understanding of the employee's current capabilities and assess any remedial actions necessary. This usually takes the form of further education.

Continuing education is a fundamental requirement for empowering employees.

The process improvement team should also assess the corporate education systems. Continuing education is a fundamental requirement for empowering employees. The effectiveness of a company's employee education system is indicative of the organization's ability to empower employees, eliminate bureaucracy, and achieve process improvement.

❖ *Document employee skills.* The current tasks require a certain set of skills. Through process improvement, it is likely that new and different skills will be required. The process improvement team needs to document the current employee skills in order to understand how they might need to change.

For each job class (or group of job classes in some cases), you can document the current skills required. Using a sample of the employee base, assess the average level of capability for that skill. Independent third-parties such as customers, suppliers, and industry analysts who have contact with your company can be good sources for external perceptions of employee skills and capabilities.

❖ *Assess the employee education systems.* If your company has a formal training department, they can be a good source of information for the process improvement team. However, other sources should be researched as well. This can include departmental budgets and actual expenditures on training. Interviews with employees will reveal their perception of training. Do employees get continuing education consistently? How many hours per year are dedicated to training? Is the training appropriate and timely for their responsibilities? Is there an established budget for education? Is the money that has been set aside for training being spent?

Employees need more than training, they need education. Training provides the employee with *how* the work is done. Education supplies *why* the work gets done. Employee empowerment is based on workers making the informed decisions that management used to make. This requires access to information and the knowledge of the "big picture" that only comes from education. It is important for the improvement team to determine how well training is providing employees with the "big picture." In particular, process members must be educated to the overall processes in which they participate.

Summary: Document and Evaluate People

- ◆ Assess effectiveness of mission and strategy.
  - – Identify the departmental missions and strategies.
  - – Identify how well the corporate mission and strategy is understood.
  - – Compare the departmental and corporate missions and strategies.

- ◆ Assess effectiveness of corporate values.
  - – Assess the formal corporate values.
  - – Identify informal corporate values.
  - – Assess informal corporate values.

- ◆ Assess change readiness.
  - – Assess commitment to change.
  - – Assess capability to change.

- ◆ Assess the effectiveness of communication systems.
  - – Assess the formal communication systems.
  - – Assess the informal communication systems.

- ◆ Assess the effectiveness of measurement and reward systems.
  - – Assess performance measures.
  - – Assess performance rewards.

- ◆ Assess employee skills.
  - – Document employee skills.
  - – Assess the employee education systems.

TPM Part 4

Conduct Benchmarking

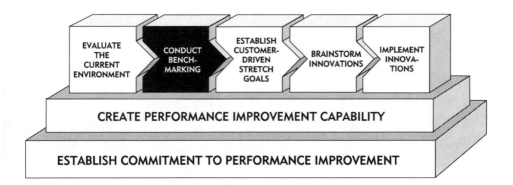

EVALUATE THE CURRENT ENVIRONMENT

CONDUCT BENCH-MARKING

ESTABLISH CUSTOMER-DRIVEN STRETCH GOALS

BRAINSTORM INNOVATIONS

IMPLEMENT INNOVA-TIONS

CREATE PERFORMANCE IMPROVEMENT CAPABILITY

ESTABLISH COMMITMENT TO PERFORMANCE IMPROVEMENT

A DOSE OF REALITY

16

Comparing Your Company to the Best

"To compare great things with small."
—Virgil

When companies find out how well other companies are doing, it often comes as a cold dose of reality. The mechanism for finding out about what our neighbors are doing is *benchmarking*. Benchmarking is an important catalyst for change and is an integral part of Total Process Management (TPM). It provides the evidence required to drive process improvement—with other companies achieving superior performance there is no longer any doubt about there being room for improvement. Benchmarking relates equally to both the process reinvention and process improvement elements of TPM. The activities in this part of the methodology are intended to contribute to the challenge performance targets for use in TPM Part 5, Establish Customer-Driven Stretch Goals.

When presented as a stand-alone methodology, benchmarking includes several elements that I cover in other Total Process Management parts. In this part, I will discuss only those elements of benchmarking not dis-cussed elsewhere in the TPM methodology. This chapter answers the question: *"What are other companies doing?"* Topics covered in this chapter include:

- ❖ Determine what to benchmark
- ❖ Develop the benchmark approach
- ❖ Select whom to benchmark
- ❖ Collect and share information
- ❖ Analyze the information

DETERMINE WHAT TO BENCHMARK

In Part 3 of the TPM methodology, Evaluate the Current Environment, we documented in substantial detail how our processes work and why certain tasks are done. In addition, we captured performance metrics related to pro-cess cycle time, cost, and quality. Benchmarking explores other companies' performance levels and the business practices that contribute to those levels. The first step in benchmarking is to determine the key business practices that structure your process. In addition to your perfor-mance metrics, these are the elements that you want to compare to other companies.

Consider the following example. An arena in which pro-cess improvement has delivered some of the most impres-sive results has been accounts payable. Restated from a TPM perspective, this is the process of "acquiring and paying for goods and services." Typically, this process cuts across several departments including purchasing, ac-

counts payable, receiving, and inventory management. In benchmarking this process, you might ask some or all of the following questions.

Metrics:

❖ How many invoices do you process? How many purchase orders?

❖ How many transactions are processed per person?

❖ What is the cost per transaction?

❖ How many vendor inquiries are processed per 1000 transactions?

❖ What is your staffing level?

❖ How long does it take in elapsed time to process a transaction?

Business Practices:

❖ How do you match purchase orders and invoices?

❖ How do you store the documents?

❖ How are receipts matched to the purchase order?

❖ Do you use any special technologies anywhere in the process?

❖ How are approvals obtained, and for what dollar amounts?

DEVELOP THE BENCHMARK APPROACH

There are several ways to conduct benchmarking. With businesses willing to cooperate, this may involve each company visiting the other and exchanging detailed operating information. In most cases, benchmarking is conducted as a survey that involves preparing a benchmark document. The primary mistake made in benchmarking documents is being unclear on what information is being requested. Some guidelines related to developing a benchmark document are:

❖ State the elements included in each category as clearly as possible.

❖ Ensure that the timeframes being considered are consistent.

❖ Indicate the unit of measure to be used in the responses related to process metrics.

❖ Use an electronic format if possible. This streamlines the recipient's efforts and makes consolidating the documents far easier.

In developing the benchmarking approach, a company must decide if it will collect the information or involve a third party such as an independent consultant. The advantages of conducting your own benchmarking effort are substantial cost savings plus the direct exposure for your employees of how other companies operate. The disadvantages are lack of expertise and the lack of independence required to obtain cooperation from competitors.

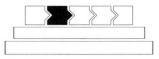

Often companies will prepare their own benchmarking document, and then hire a consultant to gather the information (to ensure confidentiality for each of the participants). A disadvantage of using outside parties is that the internal organization loses an opportunity for direct exposure to other methods of conducting business. For this reason, companies should conduct their own benchmarking whenever possible. This will capitalize on the opportunity to increase external focus and thus help build organizational enthusiasm for change.

SELECT WHOM TO BENCHMARK

Which companies should you benchmark against? Direct competitors are an obvious choice for benchmarking and should be one of your sources of information. Companies known for best-in-class performance for particular processes are an even better choice. Competitive benchmarking can help you learn your relative performance levels. Some of the benchmarked competitors will usually have superior business practices.

Companies must leap-frog their competitors' capabilities — this is the purpose of benchmarking world-class practices outside your industry.

However, copying competitor practices is a losing proposition. By the time your company has equaled a competitor's superior performance, the competitor will have introduced other improvements and your company will still be lagging behind. In this scenario, your company can never catch up.[1] The real competitive advantage comes from identifying and implementing world-class practices that none of your competitors are doing. Companies must leap-frog their competitors' capabilities — this is the strength of benchmarking world-class practices outside your industry.

Benchmarking with companies outside your industry creates some strange bedfellows. For example, Convex, the Dallas-based computer manufacturer, has looked to Chaparral Steel Company for certain business processes.[2] Many companies compare themselves to L. L. Bean Inc. for distribution processes, to Microsoft for product innovation, to Motorola for manufacturing, and to Xerox for their quality process.

The trick is finding the leading companies for the process that you are benchmarking. There are several resources for doing this. The American Society of Quality Control (ASQC) is one, as is the International Benchmark Clearinghouse, a service of the American Productivity and Quality Center. Consultants who specialize in benchmarking and professional associations are good sources of leads. Baldrige award winners, who are contractually obligated to share some of their experience with other companies, also can be good sources.

Although most benchmarking uses comparisons with competitors and world-class companies, large companies should not overlook the potential for internal benchmarking in other corporate divisions and business units. Consider the following example.

I worked with an American-based multinational company that had decided to reengineer its product development

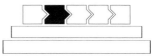

cycle. After trying in vain to locate world-class practices in competitors and in companies outside their industry, they found several great ideas in the unlikeliest place — their own company! In a routine visit to the German subsidiary, a process improvement team leader discovered that the Germans were doing several things differently. These new approaches had contributed to substantially improved customer satisfaction and to reduced costs. Here was a proven approach, perfectly suited to the home office needs that would result in significant process improvement. And it was right under their noses all along!

COLLECT AND SHARE INFORMATION

Information gathering for benchmarking is only limited by the researcher's imagination and ingenuity. In addition to information from your benchmark partners, large volumes of information are available to the public through published literature and professional associations. Customers and suppliers can be excellent sources as can joint venture partners and employees who have worked for other companies. The American Society of Quality Control is also a good information source.

Sources of published literature:

❖ Corporate financial reports
❖ Magazines and trade journals
❖ Newspapers and periodicals
❖ Books
❖ Conference materials

Sources from professional associations:

- ❖ Association reports and publications
- ❖ Association libraries
- ❖ Conferences
- ❖ Databases

After the information has been accumulated, it must be shared with each benchmarking participant. The most common approach for creating a benchmarking document is to publish a summary indicating the low, average, and high measures for each category. This maintains the anonymity of the individual contributing companies while providing valuable comparative information. Best practices generally are described in narrative format. A summary profile of the participating companies, without naming them, should be included to build credibility that the results are relevant for each company. The following example illustrates this point.

> I conducted a benchmarking exercise for a large retailer that had both branch retail stores and department stores. The chief concern of the CEO was that we compared his operations to similar operations. He asked specifically to confirm that the branch retail outlet data was compared only to branch retailers and not to department stores, and vice-versa. Had this not been done the validity and credibility of the benchmarking would have been permanently compromised.

ANALYZE THE INFORMATION

The final step is to evaluate the information for best practices that can be implemented to improve processes, to identify specific areas where the largest amount of improvement is needed, and to correct the information for inadvertent biases. Some of the adjustments required for the data include the following.[3]

❖ Appreciable differences in the scale of operations which can distort the available economies of scale.

❖ Differences in management philosophy related to centralization, outsourcing, and other concerns.

❖ Differences in product features or manufacturing processes.

❖ Disadvantages resulting from operating environments, such as cost-of-living and demographics.

After the benchmark results are complete, you are ready to move to the next step in the TPM methodology where these results are used to develop the challenge performance measures for process improvement.

TPM Part 5

Establish Customer-Driven Stretch Goals

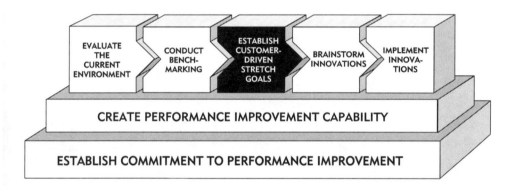

REACH FOR A STAR 17

"The ripest peach is highest on the tree."
—James Whitcomb Riley

In process improvement efforts, employees must have some idea of how much improvement needs to be obtained. Our efforts in Total Process Management Parts 3 and 4 provide the framework for setting the new performance targets. The three primary contributors to the new performance goals are customers, benchmarked companies, and executive management. Each of these contributes to performance standards along the three dimensions of speed, cost, and quality. The results of this part of the methodology are used in Part 6, Brainstorm Innovations, to provide the target performance measures.

This chapter answers the question, *"How much improvement do customers want?"* The following topics are discussed:

- ❖ Customer-Driven Stretch Performance Measures
- ❖ Challenge Performance Measures

CUSTOMER-DRIVEN STRETCH PERFORMANCE MEASURES

Corporate performance is predicated on one thing and only one thing — customers must decide that your products and services have superior value to the ones offered by the competition. Customers want to know that they can get the product or service when they want it (speed), at an acceptable price (cost), and that it delivers on its promised capabilities (quality). If you can provide these things, then you have the *potential* for strong financial performance.

Customers don't determine your *cost* for developing goods and services — they just determine what they will *pay* for them. You could sell goods at or below cost (and many companies do), but you aren't likely to stay in business for long. This is where executive management steps in. They provide the pressure to improve process *efficiency*. Efficiency is composed of two factors: resources expended and output produced. To improve efficiency, a company can reduce the resources required for a given output, increase the output for the same amount

> *In the long run men hit only what they aim at.*
>
> — *Henry David Thoreau*

246

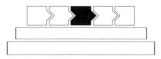

of resources, or both. For our purposes, the terms "cost" and "efficiency" are used interchangeably.

Executive management determines the desired profitability (or return on investment), which drives the efficiency levels to be achieved for the process. The benchmark information is used to support the desired performance levels. If some other company is achieving exceptional performance, your company should be able to meet or exceed those levels too — particularly if the benchmarked companies are your competition! Of course, executive management is equally concerned with speed and quality, but these are determined directly by the customer, while efficiency standards are usually determined indirectly by customers.

Figure 17.1

In the final analysis, customers drive all of a company's performance standards.

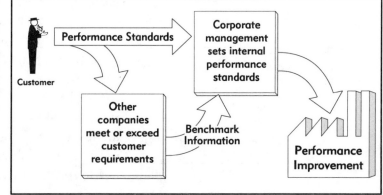

CHALLENGE PERFORMANCE MEASURES

In a recent issue, *Fortune* magazine sets out "seven steps to being the best." One of these is to *set stretch targets,* "There's nothing wrong with asking your people to perform as well as the best in the world. Don't tell them how to do it though; their ideas will be better than yours."[1] The performance targets established for your performance improvement effort should *challenge* the organization to achieve levels never before dreamed possible. Often this is necessary just to achieve the same level of performance as world-class companies.

The premise underlying Total Process Management is *transformation* of the process, with dramatic improvements in process performance. Dramatic improvements are not the sole province of process re-invention. Process value improvement also strives for dramatic improvements. Otherwise, what's the point? It just achieves the changes at a slower pace than PVR. Nobody ever achieved significant performance improvements without requiring some degree of stretch. For big improvements, this has to be a big stretch, what I call a *challenge performance measure.*

> *Climb high,*
> *Climb far.*
> *Your goal the sky,*
> *Your aim the star.*
> *—Anonymous*

Challenge performance measures force people to go beyond incremental gains to achieve remarkable improvements. This is done by setting targets so high that employees abandon any hope of continuing to fine tune the

current processes to squeeze out another 10% or 15% improvement. Challenge performance measures are derived by establishing target values *higher* than those identified from world-class best practices.

Figure 17.2

What challenge performance measures can you think of for your process?

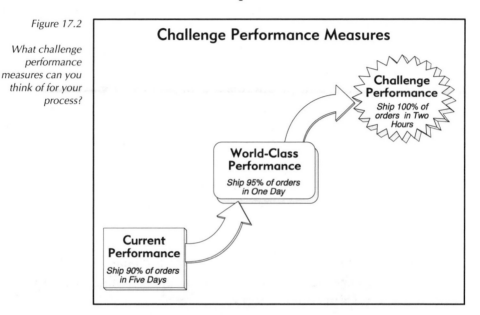

As an example, assume that your company is conducting TPM for your order fulfillment cycle. Currently it takes your company five days to ship 90% of one day's orders. The world-class practice is to ship 95% in one day—an improvement of 1500% (average 4 hours versus 60 hours). However, with our challenge performance measure, we are going to ship every order within 2 hours of when the order is received. Impossible, you say? This is an actual example of a successful project using process value reinvention. (Also, cost was reduced 45% and quality improved by 900%—all without spending a dime!) Although challenge performance measures seem absurdly unrealistic, it is this very absurdity that forces people to accept that they can no longer conduct business as usual. Another example illustrates this point.

The CEO at a global distributor for high precision automobile parts asked the process improvement team to reinvent their order fulfillment cycle. The current cycle time was 30 days. The team returned to management with recommendations that would have reduced the cycle time by a few days, but this was not enough for executive management. So, the CEO challenged the team to reach beyond their preconceived limits and achieve a cycle time of zero days. The team didn't make it to zero days, but they did reduce the cycle time down to one day! If that CEO had asked for a cycle time of 20 days (a respectable 33% reduction) what is the likelihood that the team would have achieved a one-day cycle?

Consider some of the following challenge performance measures achieved by companies though their process improvement efforts:

- ❖ An Italian bank added 50 new branches without adding any increase in personnel. Average personnel per branch dropped from seven or nine to three or four. Daily cashier closing time was reduced from over two hours to ten minutes.[2]

- ❖ At one division of AT&T, customer willingness to repurchase increased from 53% to 82%. Adjustments dropped from 4% to 0.6% of revenues, and bills paid within 30 days of installation increased from 31% to 71%.[3]

- ❖ Siemens Nixdorf Service reduced headcount by 20% while improving service technician productivity from

two to four calls per day. Overall costs were reduced by 20% as well.[4]

DIMENSIONS OF PERFORMANCE IMPROVEMENT

Performance improvement is needed in the three dimensions of speed, cost, and quality. Improvement is essential in all three categories. However, for a given process, improvement in one dimension may be more important than the others. For instance, Wal-Mart achieved process excellence through a technique called "cross-docking" that has contributed to their dominance of the competition. Cross-docking involves unloading inventory at a warehouse and then reloading it for shipment to the retail outlets without ever stocking the goods in the warehouse. This provides advantages in cycle time because goods

Figure 17.3

Customer satisfaction is driven by the combination of speed, cost, and quality.

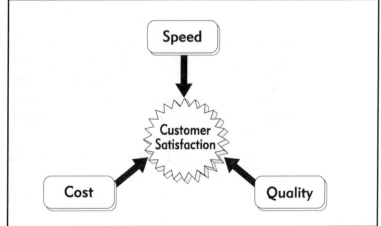

travel from the supplier to the retail store almost without stopping. However, it is not the least expensive approach. In this case, Wal-Mart's strategic advantage is derived from cycle time superiority rather than cost.[5]

Speed

The terms "speed" and "cycle time" are used interchangeably here. Cycle time is the total amount of time required to execute the process for a single transaction. It is determined by adding the elapsed times of all of the operations in the process. Recent business publications are saturated with the message of how important cycle time is to a company's competitive strength. George Stalk coined the term *time-based competition* after realizing how much faster several Japanese companies got products to market than did their U.S. competitors. He makes the point that more and more companies are gaining a competitive edge by delivering products faster than the competition.[6]

> Remember that time is money.
> — Benjamin Franklin

The majority of the cycle time for most processes is tied up in *wait time* (sometimes called *lag time* or *gap*), when no work is being performed on the transaction. The practice of executing processes in a linear fashion where one task follows another in sequence is another contributor to long cycle times. Several approaches for improving cycle time are discussed in the *Reduce Cycle Time* category of the process improvement principles (see Chapter 8). Processes where cycle time is particularly important include new product development, order fulfillment, and generation of financial reporting.

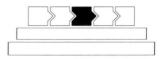

Cost

For many executives, the primary goal of process improvement is to reduce cost and, as a result, improve process efficiency. Many people believe process improvement is solely an exercise in maximizing efficiency. When introducing process improvement at companies for the first time, I am almost always asked if this is "really an exercise in efficiency with the goal to reduce headcount." Total Process Management is about meeting and exceeding customer satisfaction, and this is accomplished by improving process cycle time, quality, *and* efficiency. The Calvin and Hobbes cartoon shown in Figure 17.4 illustrates the hazards of focusing on efficiency to the exclusion of all else.

> *A billion here, a billion there, and pretty soon you're talking about real money.*
> —*Everett M. Dirksen*

Figure 17.4

Calvin shows us how focusing exclusively on efficiency can have unpleasant results.

Calvin and **Hobbes**   by Bill Watterson

With this measure we determine the cost of operating the process, usually expressed as a cost per unit of throughput. Process cost analysis, discussed in Chapter 9, is used to determine the cost of a process. Some examples of cost measures are cost per order, cost to develop a new product, and cost per customer service call.

Quality

Quality is a measure of the *effectiveness* of the process to produce products that meet customer requirements. In the TPM approach, quality is *not* the same thing as customer satisfaction. Customer satisfaction is determined by *all three* of the dimensions of performance improvement: speed, cost, *and* quality. Sample measures include amount of returned merchandise, defects per thousand units, and service ratings from customer feedback forms.

PERFORMANCE MEASUREMENT MATRIX

The primary tool for communicating the gap between the current process performance levels and the desired levels is a *performance measurement matrix*. A sample matrix is shown in Figure 17.5. As shown in the sample matrix, the speed, cost, and quality measures are displayed down the left side of the matrix. The columns across the top display the performance values for As Is, World-class, and Challenge performance measures. *As Is* measures are those of the current process. *World-class* measures are those obtained through benchmarking. *Challenge* measures are those measures *beyond* world-class that we want to achieve. This chart is used in Part 6 of the TPM methodol-

ogy, Brainstorm Innovations, as the guideline for the performance improvements required of the new process vision.

Challenge Performance Measures			
Project: PVR - New Product Delivery			
Dimension	**Current**	**World Class**	**Challenge**
Speed:			
1) Product development cycle time	3.2 yrs avg	1 yr	6 mos
2) New products per year	1	10	15
Cost:			
R&D cost per dollar of revenue	15 cents	5 cents	2.5 cents
Quality:			
1) Product test failures before shipping	5,000	500	250
2) Customer service calls	25,000/mo	8,000/mo	1,000/mo

PRESENTATION TO THE CHANGE LEADERSHIP

The final step before moving on to brainstorming innovations is to present the process improvement findings to the change leadership (one of the steering committees). The material to be presented can include some or all of the following:

❖ Proposed process mission statement
❖ Current process map
❖ Physical layout maps
❖ Span of control and organizational levels analysis
❖ Change readiness assessment

- ❖ Key business issues
- ❖ Benchmarking results
- ❖ Performance measurement matrix

This presentation serves two purposes. The first purpose for presenting the findings to the change leadership is to gain consensus for the need to change. Quite often when first implementing a change management approach, senior management grudgingly cooperates, but remains skeptical. I have never seen a skeptical senior executive that remained that way after being confronted with the information listed above. (Middle management is a different story — they often will deny even the most blatant evidence.) Consider the example below.

> I posted the process map for the order fulfillment process of one company on the wall and then showed it to the senior vice-president of sales. He was incredulous. The process map covered half of the wall and involved over 150 activities. I informed him that the cost *just to fulfill an order* was more than the *price* of several of the goods being sold, and that the process had never once achieved the performance standard of shipping 95% of one day's orders within 48 hours. Needless to say, he "saw the light" and was converted to the (drastic) need for improving the process.

The second purpose of the meeting is to reach consensus on the degree of change required. People close to the work often cannot visualize their company achieving high levels of performance, even in light of the benchmark evidence that world-class performance is not only achievable but is already being done. I have been given responses such as, "I know the other company is doing it, but our people will quit if we ask them to achieve those perfor-

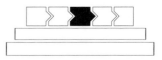

mance levels," and "they may be doing their business in a certain way, but that's not how we do it."

In cases such as these, the improvement team invariably sets lower standards — ones that they think are more realistic. Challenge performance measures *are not realistic*, and that's the entire point. You have to quite literally "think out of the box" to achieve them. The change leadership has the responsibility for pushing the process improvement team to ensure that world-class standards (or better) are set as the performance targets.

> *Challenge performance measures* are not realistic, *and that's the entire point.*

TPM Part 6

Brainstorm Innovations

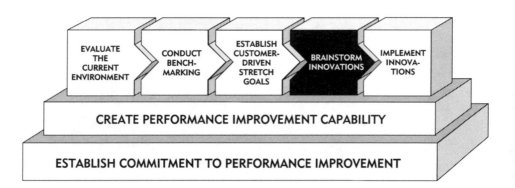

EVALUATE THE CURRENT ENVIRONMENT

CONDUCT BENCH-MARKING

ESTABLISH CUSTOMER-DRIVEN STRETCH GOALS

BRAINSTORM INNOVATIONS

IMPLEMENT INNOVA-TIONS

CREATE PERFORMANCE IMPROVEMENT CAPABILITY

ESTABLISH COMMITMENT TO PERFORMANCE IMPROVEMENT

DARE TO DREAM 18

Conducting Paradise Visioning and Focus Groups

"One can't believe impossible things,"
Alice said.
"I daresay you haven't had much
practice," said the Queen. "Why,
sometimes I've believed as many as six
impossible things before breakfast."
— Lewis Carroll

Innovation is the lifeblood of corporations. Without it, businesses slowly wither away. Innovation plays a major role in Total Process Management as well. The work leading up to this point has been mostly left-brain analytical work preparing for the big jump into right-brain thinking — what I call *paradise visioning*.[1] In this part of the methodology, the process improvement team brainstorms process innovations in order to achieve the challenge performance goals. The visioning sessions are followed by a series of focus group sessions where actions are planned to take the organization from the current environment to the new design. These *change actions* are developed through detailed planning and involvement from the organization.

Part 6 of the Total Process Management methodology answers the question, *"What ideas do we have about how to improve performance?"* It addresses the following topics:

- ❖ Cultivate an Innovation Mindset
- ❖ Conduct Paradise Visioning
- ❖ Conduct Focus Group Sessions

CULTIVATE AN INNOVATION MINDSET

What is innovation, and how do you get it? Many people think creativity is something that only certain people have. They believe that innovation means dreaming up something that has never been thought of before. If that were the case, then there would be very few innovators in the world. Here's an alternate view of creativity: innovation is the process of combining or implementing *existing* ideas and approaches in a *unique* way. This view makes innovation accessible to everyone, not just an elite few.

Discovery consists of seeing what everyone has seen and thinking what nobody has thought.

—Albert Szent-Györgyi von Nagyrapolt

At dinner recently, a colleague and I were debating the source of innovation. She maintained that a few gifted people had creative genius, and the rest of us were out of luck. She particularly liked that idea because it gave her

comfort that no one could ever expect innovation from her — she was safe knowing that she wasn't born a creative genius. I disagreed and gave her a challenge. I asked her to think of any single invention or innovation that was not based on some other phenomenon that was readily observable in some other context. In other words, you get the idea from one thing and apply to a completely unrelated area, or in an utterly unique manner. My friend tried for an hour and could not think of one and was completely disconcerted by it. She was quite annoyed to realize that she too had the same potential for innovation as supposed "geniuses."

Birds provide the context for airplanes, falling apples for gravity, and carbon paper for xerography. Even a musical prodigy such as Mozart built his music using the same musical instruments and notes that were available to everyone else; he just applied them in new ways. Make no mistake — there *are* people who have an easier time of drawing new conclusions given the same old data. However, nothing says that *everyone* cannot cultivate creativity.

At the risk of sounding like a television commercial, creativity is grounded in the ability to ask "What if?" — and not being afraid to respond with seemingly absurd answers. A mental exercise that asks the question, "What if we tried to run this business in the *worst* possible way?" can reveal how you *are* in fact running it in the worst possible way. Conversely, it can give you insights into ways to improve the current business. "What if" thinking requires the suspension of critical judgment. All too often, innovative ideas are met with ridicule or are dismissed as impractical. The process improvement team must create an environment in which crazy ideas are welcomed for what they are — seeds of innovation.

One way innovation can be achieved is to bring new people into your environment who come from a different background. For this reason, several companies in the volatile and highly competitive arena of information technology (both hardware and software) have hired new CEOs from outside the industry. Louis Gerstner at IBM and Gordon Tucker at Micrografx were hired in part to interject new ways of seeing things. For example, Tucker brings the ideas from his experiences with Procter and Gamble and PepsiCo to the world of software development and marketing.

> *It is better to know some of the questions than all of the answers.*
>
> *— James Thurber*

Another way to cultivate innovation is to look around at unrelated contexts and ask, "How can I use that idea in my area of expertise?" As one example, a leading airline studied the speed at which race car pit teams service their cars and then applied it to servicing jet airplanes.

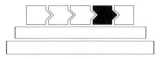

We must approach our creative brainstorming with an open and accepting mind, like that of a child. We must let go of our assumptions and sacred cows, disregard the ways we have "always done it," and think of new ways of conducting business. We need to leverage the best practices that we uncovered during benchmarking and draw on our experiences in and out of work to see things as we have never seen them.

Conduct a Creativity Workshop

In order to cultivate an innovation mindset, the first day of the visioning session should start with a "creativity workshop." The purpose of this workshop is to raise awareness of the mental blocks that prevent us from realizing our creative potential. This activity should be high energy and involve the team in exercises to get their creative juices flowing. There are many excellent books available on the subject of unlocking creative potential that are good sources for workshop material. Roger von Oech's book, *A Whack on the Side of the Head,* is a particularly good resource. One format for this creativity exercise is outlined below.

❖ Review the mental locks to creativity and discuss ways for overcoming them.

❖ Split the process improvement team into two or more groups of 5–10 people.

❖ Have each group stand around a white board or flip chart in different parts of the room. Each team will need to elect someone to write down the ideas.

❖ Give each team an everyday object as their subject (a hubcap, broom, chair, guitar, or nearly any other object will do).

❖ Ask the teams to brainstorm as many uses for the object as they can. Give them five minutes. Each idea should be written on the board for the whole team to see. The teams should work as quickly as possible. Remember, there are no wrong answers!

❖ At the end of five minutes, have the teams count the number of ideas and share them with the other groups. (This is fun. There will usually be some pretty bizarre ideas!) Declare a winner for round one (the group with the most ideas).

❖ Now comes the hard part. Have the teams brainstorm for *another* five minutes, and they cannot repeat any ideas. This is where the *really* crazy ideas start to appear.

❖ Have each team count and share their ideas, and declare a winner for round two.

This type of exercise loosens up the group and breaks through some of their inhibitions about silliness and embarrassment. It also serves as a model for the idea of *piggybacking*. This is where one idea leads to another and then to another, etc. This is one way in which crazy ideas lead to true innovation. The initial idea may be ridiculous, but it may spur an idea that is innovative *and* practical. This exercise also gets everybody involved, and sets the fast-paced tempo that is essential for non-judgmental brainstorming.

Review the Process Improvement Principles

In Chapter 8, we discussed thirty-two process improvement principles grouped in eight broad categories. The principles are used in the paradise visioning session to create the new process maps. If the team has been taught the principles, then they will probably just need a refresher of the key points. However, if they haven't been trained on the principles, then they will need this training before beginning the paradise visioning.

The process improvement team must address all of the levers for change: process, systems, structure, and people. Certain of the process improvement principles are more relevant for one of the four than for others. I have provided below my thoughts about how the process improvement principles relate to each of the four dimensions, although this certainly is not the only way. Note that some of the principles relate to more than one of the dimensions of change.

Process:

- ❖ Eliminate duplicate activities
- ❖ Combine related activities
- ❖ Eliminate reviews and approvals
- ❖ Reduce preparation
- ❖ Outsource
- ❖ Eliminate transporting
- ❖ Eliminate filing
- ❖ Create quality at the source
- ❖ Mistake proof
- ❖ Input at the source

- ❖ Create multiple process versions
- ❖ Standardize on best practices
- ❖ Use smaller batch sizes
- ❖ Implement demand pull
- ❖ Process in parallel
- ❖ Dissolve horizontal boundaries
- ❖ Change the order of activities
- ❖ Eliminate inspections

Systems:

- ❖ Outsource
- ❖ Create case managers
- ❖ Centralize/decentralize — hybridize
- ❖ Create quality at the source
- ❖ Mistake proof
- ❖ Dissolve external boundaries
- ❖ Dissolve horizontal boundaries
- ❖ Input at the source

Structure:

- ❖ Eliminate reviews and approvals
- ❖ Outsource
- ❖ Organize multi-functional teams
- ❖ Design cellular workplaces
- ❖ Create case managers
- ❖ Create case workers
- ❖ Centralize/decentralize — hybridize
- ❖ Dissolve external boundaries
- ❖ Dissolve horizontal boundaries
- ❖ Dissolve vertical boundaries

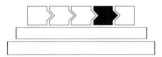

People:

- ❖ Organize multi-functional teams
- ❖ Create case managers
- ❖ Create case workers
- ❖ Create quality at the source
- ❖ Establish a teamwork culture
- ❖ Dissolve external boundaries
- ❖ Make the customer boss
- ❖ Dissolve horizontal boundaries
- ❖ Dissolve vertical boundaries
- ❖ Measure the right things
- ❖ Reward the right things
- ❖ Walk the talk
- ❖ Involve employees
- ❖ Don't pass the monkey

CONDUCT PARADISE VISIONING

After the process improvement team has been educated on the subjects discussed above, they will be ready to begin the visioning process. The sequence of events are the following:

- ❖ Review the process mission and performance measures

- ❖ Review and evaluate the current environment

- ❖ Review world-class business practices

- Conduct paradise visioning

- Document change actions

- Evaluate brainstorming effectiveness

The visioning sessions usually last from several hours (process value improvement) to several weeks (process value reinvention), depending on the scope and complexity of the processes being improved. When possible, they should take place off-site to minimize interruptions, and informal attire seems to heighten interaction and participation. Brainstorming is an intense activity. It is important to take long breaks (15 to 20 minutes) in the morning and afternoon for participants to reinvigorate themselves. Also, sending the team out for lunch can help them relax and become focused.

Review the Process Mission and Performance Measures

In Part 3 of the TPM methodology, Evaluate the Current Environment, we reviewed the congruence of the process mission with the corporate mission. If there was no process mission (which is usually the case), the team should develop one at this time. If the missions are not in harmony, revise the process mission such that it supports the corporate mission. In TPM Part 4, we established performance measures for process speed, cost, and quality. Review these with the team and develop a commitment to achieve the challenge performance measures.

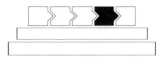

Review and Evaluate the Current Environment

Prior to beginning the session, the session facilitator should display the entire process map on the wall. The process map is usually a very large chart, so it has enormous visual shock value. Very few people (if any) understand the complete process. When confronted with the reality of a very large and complex process map, most people are astonished. This kind of sudden realization will go a long way toward building consensus around the need to improve the business process.

The process improvement team should review the process map to gain an understanding of the overall process. Any last minute corrections can be written directly onto the chart. The business issues should be discussed as well, but the team should not begin to solve them at this time. The findings related to each of the other dimensions of change (systems, structure, and people) should also be discussed.

The team may choose to conduct an exercise in order to stimulate thinking about how the current process can be changed. A sample exercise is discussed below. When done correctly, this exercise can begin to loosen the team members' hold on cherished assumptions and sacred cows.

❖ Have the team apply the process improvement principles to the current process. In particular, the team should look for activities that can be eliminated, outsourced, or combined.

❖ Have them first look for changes that require spending little or no money. This will help to identify opportunities for quick wins.

❖ Changes should be written directly onto the process map.

❖ This exercise should not take long (30 minutes to an hour). The intention is to start the innovation process, not to conduct an exhaustive exercise.

Focusing too much on the current process can be a dangerous distraction for the process improvement team. It is easy for the team to focus too much on the way things are, and simply try to fine tune the current process. It is essential for the visioning facilitator to get the team to focus on *reinventing* the process and not on maintaining the status quo. In extreme circumstances, this may involve physically removing the current process map.

Review World-Class Business Practices

Any reading materials on world-class business practices and any benchmarking results should be distributed for the team to review prior to the visioning session. Comparative benchmark material usually shows that your company is not performing competitively and serves as further confirmation of the need for dramatic improvement. At this time, you should discuss the material and brainstorm how it can be applied to the current process. Document all of the ideas generated for use in paradise visioning.

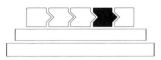

Conduct Paradise Visioning

Imagine the thrill if you were able to start over and redefine yourself, leaving out all those wrinkles, bad habits, and years of baggage! This is what paradise visioning is like, except you are imagining for your company. Here is where months of work come together and a new day is born, and just like your own birth, this experience will be painful, thrilling, and completely unique!

Paradise visioning requires large sheets or rolls of white paper. (Alternatively, the team can use process mapping software in conjunction with projection equipment so that the whole team can see.) After the blank sheets of paper are posted on the wall, begin developing the new process map. During the visioning session, reference the world-class practices, review the reengineering principles frequently, and factor in solutions for the business issues.

Paradise visioning is an exercise in dreaming.

The current process map should be referred to as little as possible to avoid the tendency to recreate the status quo. The new process should be constructed to be ideal (paradise!) *without regard for being realistic*. True innovation requires an "anything goes" approach — there will be plenty of time later to make the new ideas more realistic.

As the new process map is being developed, pay attention to each of the other dimensions of change. Ask the questions, "What new technology, facilities, and training are needed? What about new compensation systems, reporting relationships, and cultural values?" Document all of the ideas generated. The focus is on creativity and not analysis, so work quickly. Set aggressive times for measurable progress and be alert to team members who are "rooted to reality." Remember, this is an exercise in dreaming — at this stage, anything is possible!

Document Change Actions

How do we go about turning all of those pie-in-the-sky ideas into reality? This is the point in the visioning session where we begin to exercise our analytical skills. The process improvement team must determine what actions are required to make the vision a reality. This is done by comparing the current environment with the new vision and documenting each change necessary to bridge the gap. These *change actions* include a description of the change, the department(s) affected, the benefits expected, the resources required, and several other pieces of information. A sample change action is shown in Figure 18.1. The change actions serve as input to the focus group sessions where they are refined in much greater detail.

During change action definition, it is important to begin to evaluate the forces that will either act to support or prevent the action from being implemented. *Force field analysis,* which originated in the work of Kurt Lewin, is a tool that can help with this. Lewin makes the point that *driving forces* move an organization toward change while *restraining forces* block that movement. If the driving forces are stronger than the restraining forces, then the change will happen. Otherwise, it will not. With this information, the process improvement team can move to increase the driving forces and/or reduce the restraining forces. I

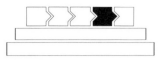

Figure 18.1

Change actions document the actions required to bridge the gap between the current and redesigned environments.

CHANGE ACTION

ID#: *CS - 01*

Change Action Name: *Institute training for Customer Service team*

Process: *Customer Service Process Value Reinvention*

Department: *Customer Service*

Prepared By: *Kent Odland*

Status: *Active*

Evaluate By: *1/5*

Person Responsible: *Monte Williams*

Start Date: *1/24*

End Date: *2/28*

Completed Date: *2/25*

---

1. Change Action Description: *CS team nees additional training to more effectively respond to customer requests. Training should be focused on areas most important to the customer. These key areas must be identified first.*

2. Estimated Resources: *Training Facilities, Trainers*

3. Improvement Principles Used: *Quality at the Source, Case Workers, Establish a Teamwork Culture*

4. Force Field Analysis:

Supports	Prevents
• *CEO very supportive of customer-oriented improvement ideas*	• *Budget constraints*
• *CS team believes that improvement is needed*	• *Department leader is resistant to change*
• *Additional training results in increased compensation*	

5. Milestones: *2/4: Define areas of highest importance to customers.*
   2/11: Create and rehearse training program.
   2/28: Complete training.

6. Expected Benefits: *A customer service team more responsive to customer needs and enabled to handle requests in a timely manner*

7. Resolution: *The team identified customer concerns via several surveys. Training program content was created by team while training services were outsourced to third-party vendor. Training of all team members concluded 3 days ahead of schedule.*

8. If late, reason for missed completion date:

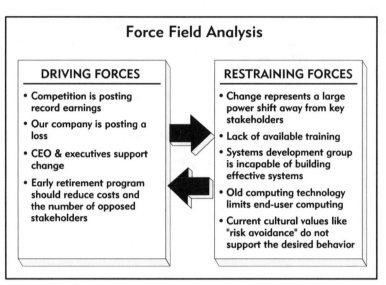

Figure 18.2

Force field analysis helps evaluate the forces that either support or prevent a change from being implemented.

Force Field Analysis

DRIVING FORCES	RESTRAINING FORCES
• Competition is posting record earnings	• Change represents a large power shift away from key stakeholders
• Our company is posting a loss	• Lack of available training
• CEO & executives support change	• Systems development group is incapable of building effective systems
• Early retirement program should reduce costs and the number of opposed stakeholders	• Old computing technology limits end-user computing
	• Current cultural values like "risk avoidance" do not support the desired behavior

favor the alternative of reducing the restraining forces because of the "ripple effect"— remove the barrier to change in one place, and it ceases to be a barrier in many other places. A sample force field analysis is shown in Figure 18.2.

Every visioning session results in a few ideas that can be implemented immediately. These "quick wins" boost employee morale and establish momentum for the improvements that take longer to achieve. It is important for the process improvement team to identify which change actions can be implemented in a very short time, and take steps to see that they are pursued.

Evaluate Brainstorming Effectiveness

In my early teens, I participated in a long distance swim meet. After swimming for nearly forever, I would look up to see if I was done. Of course, the finish line was

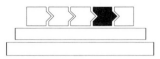

impossibly far away, so I would put my head down and swim some more. I was never so delighted as when I crossed that finish line. Visioning can seem as exhausting as a long distance swim, so your team must look up periodically to see if they have reached the performance goals. Did you achieve the challenge performance measures? If not, are you satisfied that you have done all that you can do to improve the process? If the answers to these questions are "no," then you and the other team members need to "put your heads down and swim some more." Reevaluate your progress periodically, and when you have achieved your design targets, give each other a pat on the back — you earned it!

CONDUCT FOCUS GROUP SESSIONS

The ideas generated in the visioning sessions have to work in the real world. One contributor to non-acceptance of process improvement innovations is the lack of sufficiently detailed planning. Imagine someone coming to you, beaming with self-satisfaction, and saying, "Here are five dozen great ideas — make them work!" Most people would not lift a finger to help.

The proof of the pudding is in the eating.

— Cervantes

Credibility is another barrier to getting the change actions implemented. Have your solutions considered everything involved in making the idea work? If not, you will not get much support from the organization, and the improvement will fail — it is only a matter of time. Most organizations are filled with cynics who have seen it all before. They will challenge the team with every possible exception to see if you considered them in your design. If you cannot adequately address their concerns, your solution will not be credible and your chances of gaining organizational support for the proposed changes will be low.

The detailed focus group sessions are intended to address these barriers to success. Each session should be a combination of brainstorming and detailed planning. The participants should include one or more of the original process reengineering team members, who will provide the critical element of continuity. Other participants should be employees and/or consultants who are experts in areas relating to the change action.

This is a particularly good time to involve significant stakeholders. One of the best ways to overcome organizational resistance to change is to involve as many people as possible in shaping the change. People are far more likely to accept change when they feel they had a voice in it — after all, change should be done with people, not to them.

The outcome of the focus group sessions is a detailed description of the changes that must take place to implement the change actions. Each voice should be heard in these sessions and, whenever possible, a consensus should be reached, rather than a simple majority. Facilitation by an objective third-party contributes greatly to achieving results in these sessions.

A single topic may take several sessions before resolution is reached. Ordinarily, these sessions take from four hours

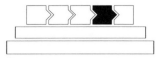

to a day, and are spaced several days apart to allow time for research and attending to ongoing responsibilities. Several different focus groups, each addressing a different topic, can be conducted at once. This substantially reduces the time ordinarily required for such detailed planning. The graphic in Figure 18.3 illustrates this point.

Figure 18.3

Usually, many focus group sessions follow the paradise visioning session.

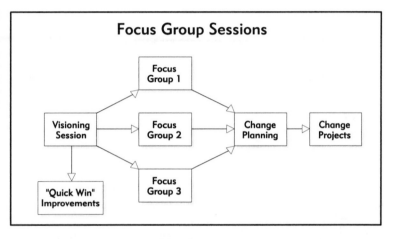

Some of the team's recommendations may involve substantial investments in capital, staff, and/or time. For example, information system development may require a large amount of funding and a cultural change program may involve a major investment in time. You can skip the focus group planning for these programs and establish them as separate projects immediately after high-level visioning.

TPM Part 7

Implement Innovations

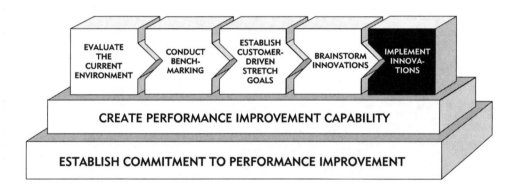

EVALUATE THE CURRENT ENVIRONMENT

CONDUCT BENCH-MARKING

ESTABLISH CUSTOMER-DRIVEN STRETCH GOALS

BRAINSTORM INNOVATIONS

IMPLEMENT INNOVA-TIONS

CREATE PERFORMANCE IMPROVEMENT CAPABILITY

ESTABLISH COMMITMENT TO PERFORMANCE IMPROVEMENT

90% DONE AND HALFWAY THERE

19

Implementing and Measuring Improvements

"Saying is one thing and doing another."
—Montaigne

By now, 90% of what we need to know to improve our processes is known, but we are less than halfway toward achieving improvement results. The best idea in the world is not worth much if it is not implemented. One of the greatest failings of creative brainstorming is lack of follow-through. In case after case, skeptical employees look at the results of brainstorming activities and wonder what's going to be different this time. They have participated in countless brainstorming sessions and poured out idea after idea only to see—nothing. So they are justifiably skeptical when someone else comes along with a new approach that is "The Answer." Accountability is not established, specific results are not committed to, and target dates are not

> The best idea in the world isn't worth much if it isn't implemented.

set. Worst of all, no one ever checks to see if any results were achieved. In this part of the Total Process Management methodology, we talk about achieving results.

Part 7 of TPM answers the question: *"How will we turn ideas into results?"* The topics covered include:

- ❖ Create Change Projects
- ❖ Develop Implementation Plans
- ❖ Track Project Progress
- ❖ Conduct a Pilot Test
- ❖ Institutionalize the Innovation

CREATE CHANGE PROJECTS

In paradise visioning, the process improvement team developed high-level change actions. These were subsequently refined into detailed change actions in the focus group sessions. Now it is time to consolidate these discrete actions into larger plans, to obtain commitments for resources, and to establish timeframes and responsibilities. In most cases, several change actions will be related in nature and can be grouped into larger implementation projects. The remainder of the change actions can be implemented individually. The determining factors are the amount of effort required for implementing the change actions, the magnitude of the impact of the innovation, and the physical resources required for implementation.

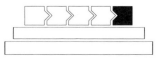

Change actions with significant scope are implemented as projects that mobilize large segments of the organization. As an example, all of the human relations changes (compensation, roles and responsibilities, performance measures, reward systems, training, and career progression) could be combined into an implementation project and addressed by a single team. Because of their scope and breadth, process reinvention efforts will almost always include one or more major change projects. Project efforts tend to be larger in scope, have greater resource requirements, and take longer to implement. Avoid projects expected to take longer than one year, or break them into smaller components with shorter timeframes. Extended projects tend to lose momentum through project team turnover, changing environmental conditions, and loss of interest.

Fig 19.1

Several change actions can be grouped into a single project.

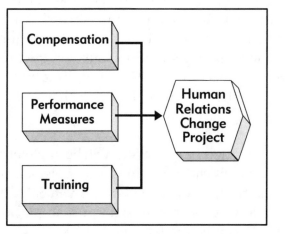

One of the first steps in implementing the innovations is to form implementation teams. These can include the process improvement team but ordinarily are not limited to them. The people who will implement the projects should come from the affected departments, the process improvement team, and possibly from external consulting firms. The chief skills required are project management ability, subject matter expertise, and knowledge of the thinking behind the recommended changes. Each major project must have a project leader to manage the project and report progress to the steering committees. High impact projects tend to be more successful when led by a key executive.

Some types of projects will be implemented with heavier representation from certain departments than others. In particular, these are systems (information systems department), structure (facilities and human resources), and people projects (human resources). It is no accident that these groups contribute some of the greatest barriers to change. (After all, the project team just committed a major trespass on their turf.) This is why it is so important to include these key support groups on the project improvement teams from the beginning. This builds their ownership of the changes and reduces their resistance to implementing the changes.

Some of the change actions will be implemented individually. Small change actions are implemented by the local workgroup or the process improvement team. These have a relatively narrow impact (for example, a single department), can be implemented quickly, and require few resources. Small change actions can usually be implemented without executive involvement.

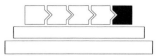

Change actions with even moderate impact generally require involving at least some degree of executive support. The executive change leaders perform several important functions with regard to the change projects. They establish priorities and coordinate change efforts, allocate resources, remove barriers to change, help sell the proposed changes to the organization, and reward the desired results.

❖ Organizations are constantly confronted with multiple opportunities competing for the same scarce investment dollars. The TPM steering committee must weigh these alternatives and select the mix of projects that best meets the company's needs.

❖ A second and no less important role of the change leadership is to coordinate change efforts. At any given time, companies will have several TPM projects, both process improvement and reinvention, underway at once. The scope and efforts of these projects must be coordinated to ensure that the results are consistent with the corporate strategy. As new projects are approved, they may overlap or supersede existing projects. The steering committee must be as quick to terminate unnecessary projects as they are to grant new ones.

❖ No matter how much you involve the organization, how empowered the workers are, how much you communicate, or how thoroughly you have analyzed the stakeholders, the proposed changes will meet with at least some resistance. The bigger the changes, the bigger the resistance. That's human nature. This is where the change leadership plays a major role. The executive sponsor and the executives on the change steering responsibility for championing the changes through the organization.

❖ Throughout the change efforts, and especially early in projects, the corporate leadership must recognize and reward improvement results. This can be done in a number of ways, including awards and recognition at company meetings and in company newsletters.

DEVELOP IMPLEMENTATION PLANS

Regardless of the size of the change project, implementation plans must be developed. These plans should be quite specific about what will be done, who will do it, when it will be done, and the resources that are required. It will be essential for every change action to be tracked through to completion — big and small alike — because without follow-up the changes simply will not materialize. Traditional project management approaches suit this need quite well. For small change actions, any tracking mechanism will do fine — I use a Lotus Notes database that allows all team members to monitor change action status. For large change projects, some form of project tracking software is essential. Two excellent personal computer-based packages are Microsoft Project and Project Workbench.

> *The difficult we do immediately. The impossible takes a little longer.*
> *— Anonymous*

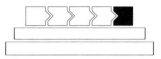

One key to effective project planning and tracking is to keep the individual project tasks to a manageable size. One rule of thumb is to create project tasks that are no longer than two weeks in duration. If these were under-estimated, the project manager will learn about it in time to take corrective action early. The same is not true of tasks that are longer than two weeks. A sample project timeline is shown in Figure 19.2.

Fig 19.2

Project timelines are an important project management tool

CHANGE PROJECT TIMELINE	Jan	Feb	Mar	Apr	May	Jun
Start-up						
Step 1						
Step 2						
Milestone						
Step 3						
Completion						

TRACK PROJECT PROGRESS

Project tracking has three key components: monitoring, reporting, and forecasting. The project leader must monitor the project to ensure that it is on schedule, on budget, and on scope. The project management software is an important tool for this. Project status is monitored through periodic reporting. The individual project teams report frequently to the project leaders (weekly or biweekly), and the project leaders report to the steering committees (usually monthly). Forecasts of impending problems are an important component of the project reporting. This information is used to modify the plans or to notify the change leadership that some proactive action may be necessary to help the project along.

The TPM and PVR steering committees should meet periodically to review the progress in implementing change actions. These regular meetings will demonstrate the committee's continued support for the project and allow committee members to intervene early if problems develop or organizational resistance surfaces.

CONDUCT A PILOT TEST

Plan, do, study, act. Anyone familiar with continuous improvement will recognize this adaptation of the Shewhart cycle. The Shewhart cycle is an improvement approach used pervasively in the quality arena, but it is equally applicable to any improvement effort, and I recommend it with TPM. A brief summary of the cycle is shown in Figure 19.3.

Plan — Analyze the current environment and brainstorm opportunities for improvement. Plan a pilot test of the change.

Do — Conduct a pilot test of the change and document the results achieved.

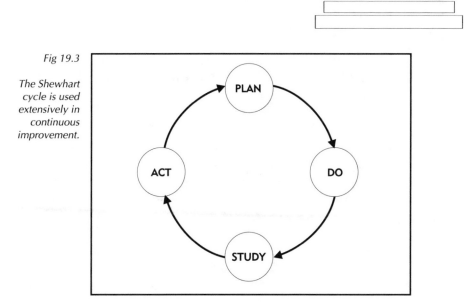

Fig 19.3

The Shewhart
cycle is used
extensively in
continuous
improvement.

Study—Study the results achieved to determine if the proposed change was successful. If not, the improvements should be modified and another test conducted.

Act—Implement the proposed changes and require the organization to standardize on the changes.

This approach has proven successful in countless companies. These steps can be found throughout the TPM methodology. We have already discussed analyzing the current environment and brainstorming innovations. In this chapter we discuss the remaining components. Whenever possible, test proposed changes using pilot tests. Not only does this help you to identify elements of the design that can be improved relatively painlessly compared to a full-scale roll out, but it builds organizational acceptance of the change as well. As people see a concept proven, it naturally becomes more acceptable to them. So, the implementation teams should execute the pilot test elements of Plan, Do, and Study. The final element of the cycle, Act, needs additional comment.

INSTITUTIONALIZE THE INNOVATION

The process improvement team has come so far. It's a shame to blow it here at the very end, but this is where many failures occur. What happens? A great improvement is implemented in some small pocket of the organization and is poorly communicated or not supported elsewhere. As a result, few real results are achieved, if any at all. The solution is to standardize on the practice throughout the process. This requires communication and training — perpetually.

Process members must be in a constant state of learning about changes to the process.

Let me say that again. The process members must be in a constant state of learning about changes to the process. Why? Because processes change constantly. The only way for empowerment to work is for employees to understand the big picture, and how their individual efforts impact the entire process. When changes directly affect an individual's work, specific training will be needed. Otherwise, the process members may simply need timely communication of changes.

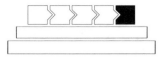

There is one way and only one way for people participating in a process to visualize the entire process — a process flowchart or process map. Every employee must have access to the flowcharts of the processes to which they contribute. In addition, these flowcharts must be updated as appropriate and the changes communicated to all of the process members. Otherwise, all these wonderful changes we have worked so hard to achieve will soon be ground to dust by the organizational gristmill.

CONCLUSION

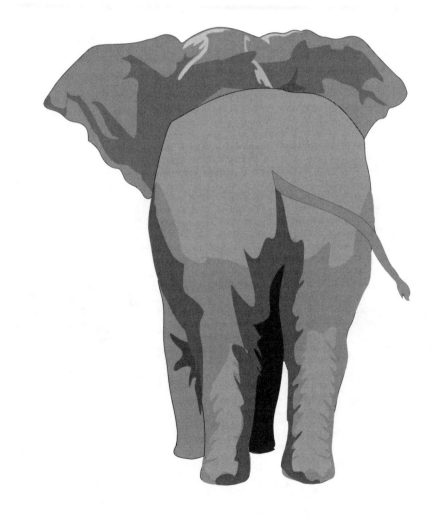

WORKING IN A HORIZONTAL WORLD 20

Business in the Year 2000

Enter the year 2000—a time where constant change is the only thing we can count on consistently. Work as we know it will be very different and those who adapt to the changing environment will have tremendous opportunities for success. What are some trends of the new workplace?

❖ The size of larger companies will diminish while small firms will purposefully stay small.

❖ The hierarchical organization will give way to the more flexible and responsive network structure.

❖ The worker will be rediscovered as an asset to be cultivated instead of an expense to be managed.

❖ Process management will supersede functional management as the best method for satisfying the customer.

With these ideas in mind, let's take a step toward the future and see what's out there.

COMPANIES GET SMALL

We have all heard the buzzwords: downsizing, rightsizing, and streamlining. Whatever the euphemism, the bottom line is that companies are getting smaller. IBM, with a work force of 406,000 in 1985, was around 302,000 in late 1993. Likewise, DEC's population dropped over 20% from 126,000 in 1989 to the current 98,000. These giants in the undisputed growth industry of computer technology are competing with the lighter and leaner Apples (15,100 employees), Microsofts (13,800) and Novells (3,500) of the world.[1]

If you think this contraction is a temporary phenomenon, think again. According to MIT researchers, while the average number of company employees increased until the 1970s, it has been ever decreasing since then, especially in manufacturing.[2] What are some of the reasons for this trend? One key factor is the sheer power of technology. While experts argue the specifics, most agree that the sum total of scientific knowledge has been doubling every six to ten years since the 1960s. This technology is enabling fewer people to do more than ever before. Researchers found that while an average company eliminated 20% of its employees over a ten-year period, it increased its investment in information technology by 300%.[3]

Companies are shrinking and becoming more tightly focused on their primary business.

Another important factor is outsourcing. Farming out nonessential activities that others can do faster and/or cheaper allows companies to focus on their "core competencies" and do what they do best. For a traditional example, a leading manufacturer of industrial aluminum may hire a company to handle all of its data processing needs concerning payroll or accounts receivable instead of investing in the resources required to manage this on its own. However, the term "nonessential activities" is relative. MCI, for example, has taken the concept a step farther to include outsourcing all research and development. Over 9000 engineers, none of which is on the company payroll, support all of MCI's research and development activities.[4]

So companies are shrinking and becoming more tightly focused on their primary business. How does this shift affect the corporate structure? Let's take a look.

HIERARCHIES COLLAPSE

Picture a spider web. It is light and flexible, and each strand is connected to another one. This is a picture of the network organization and it is very different from the pyramid-like corporate structures dominating the land today. No longer will a customer wait for a salesperson to wait for a boss to check with another functional department on the feasibility of a custom order. Technology allows information to be shared by all instead of controlled by managers. Telecommunication connects those who need expertise with those who have it.

While the concept of self-managed teams is not new (it was "discovered" by a researcher in an English coal mine in 1949), the impact on corporate organization is profound.[5] The need for command and control supervision disappears as tasks normally performed by management are now the cross-functional team's responsibility. Not only does the team handle issues such as scheduling and production, but also administrative ones like evaluating, hiring, and firing as well. Productivity increases of 40% are not uncommon in this environment.[6]

So what is the role of the manager in this networked and self-managed brave new world? First of all, a name change is in order. Titles such as facilitator, mentor, or coordinator more closely define this person's responsibilities in the future. As Motorola puts it, a manager must be "a guide on the side instead of a sage on the stage."[7] These specialists will be paid not for making snap decisions, but for coordinating the efforts of teams and individuals both internal and external to the company into a seamlessly aligned effort toward strategic corporate goals.

A manager must be a "guide on the side instead of a sage on the stage."[7]

New structures. New roles. Ultimately even the way we think about work is changing at breakneck speed.

FOCUSING ON THE WORKER

As the enabling power of technology allows people to spend less time on routine work like validating and collecting information, people are freed to spend more time planning for the future. "Thought leaders" will devote their efforts to envisioning new ways to improve a process, satisfy a customer, or incorporate a new technology.

Learning itself will take on a whole new importance as companies shift from considering employees as "costs to be cut" to "assets to be developed."[8] Creating a learning organization through job rotation and continuing education replaces controlling the organization as a primary function of management. A GE plant in Puerto Rico that manufactures surge protectors for power stations and transmission lines is doing just this with amazing results. Hourly team members earn raises and bonuses by rotating jobs regularly (to understand their impact on the next person in the process), specializing in a particular machine or functional skill, and meeting plant-wide goals for performance and attendance. After one year in operation, the plant was 20% more productive than any company equivalent in the U.S., and predictions were that productivity would rise another 20% by the end of 1993.[9]

The question shifts from "Who reports to you?" to "What can you do?"

Specialization is a natural result of striving to stay on top of the constantly changing technological heap. The question shifts from "Who reports to you?" to "What can you do?" Likewise, compensation will be tied less to position or seniority and more to the ever-changing market value of a particular set of skills.

With increased specialization comes the rise of a new and largely unnoticed category of the labor force — the technical worker. This category does not quite fit the normal white collar or blue collar mold. They have titles such as Medical Technologist, Paralegal, and Computer Technician. Their numbers are growing. While currently comprising 16% of the work force, experts predict that their ranks could swell to 20% or 23 million people by the year 2000 — the largest segment of the working population.[10]

However, increased employee development and specialization can only take us so far if the paradigm of how we work remains unchanged.

MANAGING THE PROCESS

In the old world, the Research and Development (R&D) department developed a prototype and tossed it over the functional wall to manufacturing, who decided how to build it. Manufacturing then threw the finished product over to sales and marketing, whose job it was to sell it. Every snag along the way resulted in the problem being pitched back over the wall and delayed until "they" fixed it. Long cycle times, increased rework, and compromised quality were just a few of the inherent problems vertical management caused.

Enter the new world. Horizontal teams of specialists from each of the affected functional areas work together and are responsible for ultimately delivering a specific good or service to the customer. At Hallmark, members of the Christmas Team or the Valentine's Day Team are writers, artists, lithographers, accountants, and marketers.[11] By sitting together and interactively exchanging ideas with each other, potential problems or innovative ideas can be identified up front, instead of downstream when it is often very costly to make improvements.

Michael Hammer has this to say about the future: "You no longer have a box on an organization chart. You'll own part of a process map."[12] With process ownership comes a new sense of pride and responsibility to the customer. Blaming the "other department" and saying "That's not my job" disappear as team members understand the entire process and can make changes to improve it.

Understanding and owning a process leads to a profound shift from trying to please the boss to doing everything possible to satisfy the customer. Rank on the corporate ladder no longer defines authority when dealing with customers. The process specialist on the phone with the customer must be able to resolve his issues without depending on a supervisor to authorize a $2,000 question and his supervisor's supervisor to authorize a $5,000 question. In these days, the customer just won't wait.

And so ends our look into the workplace of the future. We have talked about change and the opportunity that accompanies that change. The organizations and individuals who embrace change as a natural and needed part of life will flourish while those who do not, will not. So the final question is:

Which one will you be?

THE MALCOLM **A**
BALDRIGE
NATIONAL
QUALITY AWARD

The Malcolm Baldrige National Quality Award, like most American quality movements, can be traced back to the early 1980s. Concerned about declining U.S. global market position, leaders from government and industry formed the American Productivity and Quality Center (APQC) in 1983. The APQC sponsored quality and productivity conferences and ultimately recommended creating a national quality award much like Japan's coveted Deming Prize, named for the quality luminary W. Edwards Deming in 1951.

Initial legislation was introduced in August, 1986, and was strongly supported by then Secretary of Commerce, Malcolm Baldrige. The bill was reintroduced in January, 1987, and when Baldrige unexpectedly died in June, the legislation was renamed in his honor and quickly gained momentum. Ronald Reagan signed the Malcolm Baldrige National Quality Improvement Act in August, 1987, and the race for quality began.

The purpose of the Award is to promote U.S. quality and productivity by:

❖ Encouraging companies to achieve excellence for the pride of achievement.

❖ Recognizing world-class companies to provide examples to others.

❖ Creating guidelines that any organization can use to evaluate and improve their own quality system.

❖ Disseminating information from winning companies on managing for excellent quality.

By far, the most important use for the Award is for purposes of self-assessment. It is crucial to know where your company ranks with competitors and the "best of breed" in terms of quality. The National Quality Award provides an excellent benchmark from which to compare.

Information sharing is another important aspect of the Award. Winners are contractually obligated to share quality strategies with all interested parties in the spirit of fostering quality improvement nationwide. While the degree of sharing is not specifically defined, the open information exchange has been far greater than originally anticipated.

Finally, the Award has the affect of accelerating existing quality initiatives. The National Quality Award is an integrated and comprehensive checklist of all quality issues necessary for a successful quality system. Xerox, for one, firmly asserts that the Award criteria advanced their quality effort by 3–4 years.

Applicants may apply for the National Quality Award in one of three areas: manufacturing, small business, or service. A maximum of two winners for each category is allowed; however, if no company meets the strict criteria, no award is presented. In fact, from 1988 to 1993, only 19 of 36 awards were given in the three areas: manufacturing (11), small business (5), and service (3).

The Award consists of seven examination categories which total a maximum of 1,000 points. The categories are:

Leadership	90	points
Information and Analysis	80	points
Strategic Quality Planning	60	points
Human Resources	150	points
Quality Assurance	140	points
Quality Results	180	points
Customer Satisfaction	300	points
TOTAL	**1,000**	points

A 1991 General Accounting Office (GAO) study examined 1988 and 1989 Award applicants to determine what impact the relentless pursuit of quality would have on performance. Overall, these companies improved in four measurable areas: employee relations, operating procedures, customer satisfaction, and financial performance. The three examples discussed below support this conclusion.

In 1986, Motorola, Inc., a leading electronics manufacturer, pushed its pursuit of total quality into high gear by setting the unheard of goal of "6 sigma" quality. For the 1988 Award winner, that meant only 3.4 defects per million parts or 99.9999998% perfect products. Cycle time in the cellular phone division is down 30 to 1 with defects falling 90%. The semiconductor area has seen shipping errors drop 53% as well. However, quality improvements are not just limited to the shop floor. Motorola patent lawyers used to take from 19 to 36 months to write and file a patent claim. The time required has been reduced to two months and the 6 sigma goal is one day.[1]

Milliken & Company, a privately owned textile and chemical firm, turned to quality as a means of fighting off fierce foreign competition. On-time delivery jumped from 75% in 1984 to 99% (the industry best) in 1988 when they won the Award. An employee suggestion system that yielded 0.5 ideas per associate at its inception, swelled to 39.3 ideas per associate in 1990 with a completion rate of 85%. Total number of suppliers was reduced by 72% while 1989 sales surged from $1 billion to $2 billion in 1990.[2]

Xerox Corporation, a 1989 Award winner, got a wake-up call in the late 1970s after discovering that its Japanese counterparts were selling copiers for less than Xerox could manufacture them. Survival meant making quality a basic business principle for the company—and fast. From 1984 to 1989, defects per 100 machines decreased by 78% while unscheduled maintenance dropped 40%. Xerox cut its supplier base from 5,000 to 400 over a nine-year period while its market share grew from 9% in 1980 to 16% in 1991. Customer satisfaction is up 38% and Xerox now has more pleased customers than any other company in the middle to high volume copier market.[3]

Despite remarkable success stories such as these, the number of companies applying for the Award has declined in successive years since 1991. Some people speculate that the reason is a growing belief that TQM is a dying fad.[4] Although there is clearly some truth to that perception that TQM fails more often than it succeeds, there is another explanation of the decline in Baldrige applicants rooted in the success of TQM. Many of the TQM leaders (some of which are Baldrige winners) require of their suppliers that they be capable of applying for the Award. As these TQM leaders applied the process improvement principles, they gradually reduced the number of suppliers — in some cases dramatically. This fewer number of suppliers could be one reason that applications have declined.

The quality movement is not a flash in the pan. Neither is it a source of sustainable competitive advantage. Quality is a prerequisite for survival — pure and simple. The Malcolm Baldrige National Quality Award allows any organization to assess its position against key criteria necessary to become world-class and provides a blueprint for creating a quality culture tailored specifically to the organization's specific needs.

For more information on the Malcolm Baldrige National Quality Award or for a free copy of the Application Guidelines, please contact:

Malcolm Baldrige National Quality Award
National Institute of Standards
and Technology
Route 270 and Quince Orchard Road
Administration Building, Room A 537
Gaithersburg, Maryland 20899
(301) 975-2000

ISO 9000

The International Organization for Standardization (ISO) is a global body committed to promoting the development of standards, quality testing, and quality certification in order to facilitate trade of goods and services worldwide. ISO consists of representatives from 91 countries. The U.S. representative to ISO is the American National Standards Institute (ANSI).

ISO 9000 is the collective title for five international standards on quality management and compliance. The guidelines evolved from existing quality standards. For example, ISO 9000 incorporates the MIL-Q 9858A standard from the U.S. Department of Defense as well as aspects of the British standard BS 5750 and NATO's AQAP 1 standard.

The ISO standards include ISO 9000, 9001, 9002, 9003, and 9004. ISO 9000 is a reference document used as a guide to select the appropriate internal or external compliance standards. ISO 9001, 9002, and 9003 are the actual certification components of the ISO series that deal with supplier conformance to customer requirements on a contractual basis (external compliance). Finally, ISO 9004 provides guidance in establishing a basic quality management system (internal compliance).

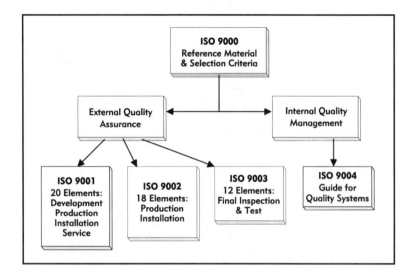

ISO 9000. This document provides guidance for selecting among ISO 9001, 9002, and 9003 for the appropriate standard for each particular company and situation. It also defines the ISO 9000 standard concepts and terminology.

ISO 9001. This standard is the most comprehensive of the external compliance standards. It contains all 20 of the quality system elements and is the standard for quality assurance in design/development, production, installation, and servicing.

ISO 9002. This document contains 18 of the quality elements and is used primarily for conformance to quality requirements related to production and installation.

ISO 9003. This is the least comprehensive of the standards and therefore easiest to implement. It contains 12 quality system elements and is used when compliance to standards is required only for final inspection and test.

ISO 9004. This standard is a reference document that presents the basic elements necessary to design and implement a quality-management system. ISO 9004 is useful for companies that do not have a quality-management system. It is also intended for companies that have a quality system and want to bring it more in line with the ISO format.

The fundamental premise behind the ISO 9000 series is that the products and/or services of certified companies conform to quality requirements. There are three primary ways in which a company can certify under ISO 9000.

❖ Self-certification
❖ Second-party certification
❖ Third-party certification

Self-certification occurs when the supplier declares that it is meeting ISO 9000 quality standards. With this approach, there is no independent verification of conformance to ISO 9000 standards. An advantage of this method is that the company controls the entire process, which reduces time and costs. The primary disadvantage is that the certification may not be recognized by customers, which would undermine the usefulness of having the certification.

Second-party certification requires the customer to audit the supplier and certify that the quality standards are being met. This option has the advantage of allowing the supplier to customize the system to a specific customer's requirements. However, in customizing quality assurance for one customer, the supplier may reduce its chances for the certification to be recognized by other customers. These customers may require their own audit, which adds to cost and time requirements.

Third-party certification occurs when the supplier's quality assurance system is reviewed by a third party registrar. Upon approval, the registrar places the supplier on a register with other suppliers that successfully completed certification. The main advantage of this approach is an internationally recognized quality system. The disadvantage is that this approach is costly. It requires a large amount of effort and resources to develop, achieve, and sustain the certification.

ISO 9000 certification is not an inexpensive process, although the benefits can be worth it. A survey of 1,700 ISO 9000-registered firms in North America revealed that companies spend $245,000 on average to achieve certification. Companies recover these costs in an average of three years, with annual savings averaging from $25,000 for small firms to $500,000 for large firms. However, the payoff comes in more than cost savings. One of the top reasons for ISO 9000 is customer-driven expectations. In fact, over 95% of the companies surveyed said they planned to use their certification for public-relations purposes.[1]

Most ISO 9000 experts agree that ISO 9000 will be the globally accepted standard within the near future. Two recent examples support this trend.

❖ In 1990, the U.S. Food and Drug Administration (FDA) announced its intention to replace its Good Manufacturing Practices (GMP) standards with ISO 9001 and additional requirements.

❖ In 1991, Japan's Ministry of Industry and Trade (MITI) committed to adopting ISO 9000. Also, regulatory agencies of North America, the Pacific Rim, and Europe plan to standardize certification and testing requirements for pharmaceutical products.

An ISO committee recommended four strategic goals to carry quality system certification into the future. The report, which is titled *Vision 2000*, addresses the following areas.

❖ *Obtain Universal Acceptance*. ISO 9000 is defined broadly so that it can be applied to any organization, from manufacturing and service companies to local government and public schools.

❖ *Maintain Current Compatibility*. Document numbering for all of the ISO standards will be consistent.

❖ *Assure Forward Compatibility*. Future revisions will be consistent in language and document numbering to allow easy assimilation for companies already using ISO 9000.

❖ *Guarantee Forward Flexibility*. Future revisions will be minor and will be implemented gradually in order to avoid invalidating any existing contractual obligations between suppliers and customers.

ISO 9000 is not a total quality management system. It is, however, a series of standards that can only be met through a solid quality assurance system. For further information on ISO 9000, contact the American National Standards Institute at the address shown below.

ANSI
11 West 42nd Street
New York, New York 10036
(212) 642-4900

NOTES

Chapter 1

1. "How Will We Live with the Tumult?", Stratford Sherman, *Fortune*, December 13, 1993, p. 123.
2. "Managing Change: The Art of Balancing," Jeanie Daniel Duck, *Harvard Business Review*, November–December 1993, p. 109.
3. *Quality Digest*, November 1993, p. 13.
4. "Paradigms for Postmodern Managers," John A. Byrne, *Business Week*, Reinventing America 1992, p. 62.
5. "ASAP Interview with Michael Hammer," *Forbes ASAP*, 1993, p. 75.
6. "Rising Stars," Michael H. Mescon and Timothy S. Mescon, *Sky*, June 1993.
7. "A Master Class in Radical Change," Stratford Sherman, *Fortune*, December 13, 1993, p. 83.
8. "Management Tools and Techniques: An Executive Guide," Bain & Company and the Planning Forum, 1994.
9. "Reengineering: The Hot New Managing Tool," Thomas A. Stewart, *Fortune*, August 23, 1993, p. 41.
10. "Successful Change Programs Begin with Results," Robert H. Schaffer and Harvey A. Thompson, *Harvard Business Review*, January–February 1992, p. 81.
11. "Strategic Intent," Gary Hamel and C. K. Prahalad, *Harvard Business Review*, May–June 1989, p. 67.
12. "Managing Change: The Art of Balancing," Jeanie Daniel Duck, *Harvard Business Review*, November–December 1993, p. 109.
13. "Many Companies Try Management Fads, Only to See Them Flop," Fred R. Bleakley, *Wall Street Journal*, July 6, 1993, p. 1.
14. "Successful Change Programs Begin with Results," Robert H. Schaffer and Harvey A. Thompson, *Harvard Business Review*, January–February 1992, p. 84.

Chapter 2

1. "ASAP Interview with Michael Hammer," *Forbes ASAP*, 1993, p. 70.
2. "A Master Class in Radical Change," Stratford Sherman, *Fortune*, December 13, 1993, pp. 82–83.
3. "The Core Competence of the Corporation," Gary Hamel and C. K. Prahalad, *Harvard Business Review*, May–June 1990, p. 80.

4. "A Company of Business People," John Case, *Inc.*, April 1993, p. 81.
5. Ibid., p. 89.
6. "The Horizontal Company," John A. Byrne, *Business Week*, December 20, 1993, p. 77.
7. "Many Companies Try Management Fads, Only to See Them Flop," Fred R. Bleakley, *Wall Street Journal*, July 6, 1993, p. 1.
8. "The New Computer Revolution," Stratford Sherman, *Fortune*, June 14, 1993, p. 58.
9. "Rethinking IBM," Judith H. Dobrzynski, *Business Week*, October 4, 1993, p. 88.
10. "The Horizontal Corporation," John A. Byrne, *Business Week*, December 20, 1993, pp. 76–77.

Chapter 3

1. H. James Harrington, *Business Process Improvement*, (McGraw-Hill, 1991).
2. "Copycats," David Altany, *Industry Week*, November 5, 1990, p. 12.
3. "Benchmarking: The Search for Best Practices That Lead to Superior Performance," Robert C. Camp, *Quality Progress*, January 1989, p. 64.
4. "Copycats," David Altany, *Industry Week*, November 5, 1990, p. 12.
5. "Benchmarking: Lessons from the Best-in-Class," Rick Whiting, *Electronic Business*, October 7, 1991, p. 132.
6. "Many Companies Try Management Fads, Only to See Them Flop," Fred R. Bleakley, *Wall Street Journal*, July 6, 1993, p. 1.
7. "Compressing Time to Market: Today's Competitive Edge," George Weimer, Bernie Knill, James Manji, and Beverly Beckert, *Industry Week*, May 4, 1992, p. 11.
8. "Strategic Intent," Gary Hamel and C. K. Prahalad, *Harvard Business Review*, May–June 1989, p. 63.
9. "Are you as Good as the Best In the World?", Joyce E. Davis, *Fortune*, December 13, 1993, p. 95.
10. "Reengineering: The Hot New Managing Tool," Thomas A. Stewart, *Fortune*, August 23, 1993, p. 41.
11. "A Master Class in Radical Change," Stratford Sherman, *Fortune*, December 13, 1993, p. 83.
12. "GM Gets A Tune-up," Alex Taylor III, *Fortune*, November 29, 1993, p. 56.
13. "TQM: More than a Dying Fad?" Rahul Jacob, *Fortune*, October 18, 1993. p. 66.
14. Ibid.
15. Ibid., p. 67.
16. "When Times Get Tough, What Happens to TQM?" Daniel Niven, *Harvard Business Review*, May–June 1993, p. 21.
17. "A Master Class in Radical Change," Stratford Sherman, *Fortune*, December 13, 1993, p. 88.
18. "TQM: More than a Dying Fad?" Rahul Jacob, *Fortune*, October 18, 1993. p. 66.
19. "Reengineering Work: Obliterate, Don't Automate," Michael Hammer, *Harvard Business Review*, July–August 1990, p. 107.
20. Tom Peters, *Liberation Management*, (New York: Alfred A. Knopf, 1992), p. 101.
21. "Reengineering: The Hot New Managing Tool," Thomas A. Stewart, *Fortune*, August 23, 1993, p. 43.

22. "How to Make Reengineering Really Work," Gene Hall, Jim Rosenthal, and Judy Wade, *Harvard Business Review*, November–December 1993, p. 119.
23. "Reengineering: The Hot New Managing Tool," Thomas A. Stewart, *Fortune*, August 23, 1993, p. 42.
24. Ibid.
25. "A Master Class in Radical Change," Stratford Sherman, *Fortune*, December 13, 1993, p. 88.
26. "Re-Engineering Gives Firms New Efficiency, Workers the Pink Slip," Al Ehrbar, *Wall Street Journal*, March 16, 1993.
27. Michael Hammer and James Champy, *Reengineering the Corporation*, (New York: HarperCollins Publishers, Inc., 1993), p. 49.
28. "Reengineering: The Hot New Managing Tool," Thomas A. Stewart, *Fortune*, August 23, 1993, p. 48.
29. Dr. Michael Hammer, *Understanding Reengineering*, (Hammer and Company, 1993).
30. "The Next Quality Imperative," Karl Albrecht, *Quality Digest*, November 1993, p. 19.

Chapter 4

1. "The New Computer Revolution," Stratford Sherman, *Fortune*, June 14, 1993, p. 56.
2. "GM Gets A Tune-Up," Alex Taylor III, *Fortune*, November 29, 1993, p. 56.
3. "Staple Yourself to an Order," Benson P. Shapiro, V. Kasturi Rangan, and John J. Sviokla, *Harvard Business Review*, July–August 1992 p. 116.
4. "A Company of Business People," John Case, *Inc.*, April 1993, p. 82.
5. "Paradigms for Postmodern Managers," John A. Byrne, *Business Week*, Reinventing America 1992, p. 63.
6. Stephen R. Covey, *The Seven Habits of Highly Effective People*, (New York: Simon & Schuster, Inc., 1989), p. 359.
7. "Competing on Capabilities: The New Rules of Corporate Strategy," George Stalk, Philip Evans, and Lawrence E. Shulman, *Harvard Business Review*, March–April 1992, pp. 61–62.
8. Ibid., p. 62.
9. Ibid.
10. "A Master Class in Radical Change," Stratford Sherman, *Fortune*, December 13, 1993, p. 84.
11. "The Horizontal Corporation," John A. Byrne, *Business Week*, December 20, 1993, p. 79.
12. "Paradigms for Postmodern Managers," John A. Byrne, *Business Week*, Reinventing America, 1992, p. 63.
13. "A Master Class in Radical Change," Stratford Sherman, *Fortune*, December 13, 1993, p. 84.
14. "The Horizontal Corporation," John A. Byrne, *Business Week*, December 20, 1993, p. 77.
15. "Management's New Gurus," John A. Byrne, *Business Week*, August 31, 1992, p. 46.
16. "Payoff from the New Management," Brian Dumaine, *Fortune*, December 13, 1993, p. 103.
17. "The Horizontal Corporation," John A. Byrne, *Business Week*, December 20, 1993, p. 78.
18. "Looking Beyond the Costs," Bruce Caldwell, *Information Week*, January 3, 1994, p. 52.

19. "A Master Class in Radical Change," Stratford Sherman, *Fortune*, December 13, 1993, p. 88.
20. "Competing on Capabilities: The New Rules of Corporate Strategy," George Stalk, Philip Evans, and Lawrence E. Shulman, *Harvard Business Review*, March–April 1992, p. 57.
21. "Rate Your Readiness to Change," Thomas A. Stewart, *Fortune*, February 7, 1994, p. 106.
22. Ibid.

Chapter 5

1. "TQM: More than a Dying Fad?", Rahul Jacob, *Fortune*, October 18, 1993, p. 72.
2. Paradise Visioning is loosely based on the term "Paradise Principle" used in the Price Waterhouse change methodology called Business Process Transformation.
3. "Reengineering: The Hot New Managing Tool," Thomas A. Stewart, *Fortune*, August 23, 1993, p. 41.
4. "TQM: More than a Dying Fad?", Rahul Jacob, *Fortune*, October 18, 1993, p. 66.

Chapter 6

1. "Reengineering: The Hot New Managing Tool," Thomas A. Stewart, *Fortune*, August 23, 1993, p. 48.
2. Ibid., p. 47.
3. "How to Make Reengineering Really Work," Gene Hall, Jim Rosenthal, and Judy Wade, *Harvard Business Review*, November–December 1993, p. 124.
4. "A Master Class in Radical Change," Stratford Sherman, *Fortune*, December 13, 1993, p. 84.
5. "Reengineering: The Hot New Managing Tool," Thomas A. Stewart, *Fortune*, August 23, 1993, p. 42.
6. "Reengineering Aetna," Glenn Rifkin, *Forbes ASAP*, p. 81.
7. "A Master Class in Radical Change," Stratford Sherman, *Fortune*, December 13, 1993, p. 88.
8. "How to Make Reengineering Really Work," Gene Hall, Jim Rosenthal, and Judy Wade, *Harvard Business Review*, November–December 1993, p. 128.
9. Ibid., p. 124.
10. "TQM: More than a Dying Fad?" Rahul Jacob, *Fortune*, October 18, 1993, p. 67.
11. Ibid., p. 68.
12. "How to Make Reengineering Really Work," Gene Hall, Jim Rosenthal, and Judy Wade, *Harvard Business Review*, November–December 1993, p. 129.
13. "A Master Class in Radical Change," Stratford Sherman, *Fortune*, December 13, 1993, p. 84.
14. Ibid., p. 83.
15. Ibid., p. 84.
16. "Revolutionize Your Company," Noel M. Tichy, *Fortune*, December 13, 1993, p. 115.
17. "A Master Class in Radical Change," Stratford Sherman, *Fortune*, December 13, 1993, p. 83.

18. Ibid., p. 90.
19. "Reengineering: The Hot New Managing Tool," Thomas A. Stewart, *Fortune*, August 23, 1993, p. 43.
20. "How to Make Reengineering Really Work," Gene Hall, Jim Rosenthal, and Judy Wade, *Harvard Business Review*, November–December 1993, p. 128.
21. "A Master Class in Radical Change," Stratford Sherman, *Fortune*, December 13, 1993, p. 84.
22. "Managing Change: The Art of Balancing," Jeanie Daniel Duck, *Harvard Business Review*, November–December 1993, p. 111.
23. "How to Make Reengineering Really Work," Gene Hall, Jim Rosenthal, and Judy Wade, *Harvard Business Review*, November–December 1993, p. 130.
24. "Managing Change: The Art of Balancing," Jeanie Daniel Duck, *Harvard Business Review*, November–December 1993, p. 112.
25. Stephen R. Covey, *The Seven Habits of Highly Effective People*, (New York: Simon & Schuster, Inc., 1989), p. 240.
26. "Getting beyond Downsizing," Ronald Henkoff, *Fortune*, January 10, 1994, p. 64.
27. Ibid.
28. "Reengineering Gives Firms New Efficiency, Workers the Pink Slip," Al Ehrbar, *Wall Street Journal*, March 16, 1993.
29. "Getting beyond Downsizing," Ronald Henkoff, *Fortune*, January 10, 1994, p. 64.
30. "Successful Change Programs Begin with Results," Robert H. Schaffer and Harvey A. Thompson, *Harvard Business Review*, January–February 1992, p. 85.

Chapter 7

1. "Getting Beyond Downsizing," Ronald Henkoff, *Fortune*, January 10, 1994, p. 58.
2. SHRM/Saratoga Institute, *1991 Human Resources Effectiveness Report*, (Saratoga Institute, 1991)
3. Stephen R. Covey, *The Seven Habits of Highly Effective People*, (New York: Simon & Schuster, Inc., 1989), p. 54.
4. "TQM: More that a Dying Fad," Rahul Jacob, *Fortune*, October 18, 1993, p. 68.
5. Ibid.
6. Ibid.
7. Ibid.

Chapter 9

1. "A New Tool for Managing Costs," Terence P. Pare, *Fortune*, June 14, 1993, p. 126.

Chapter 10

1. Roger von Oech, *A Whack on the Side of the Head*, (Warner Books, 1983), p. 114.
2. Ibid., p. 11.

Chapter 15

1. "Are You as Good as the Best in the World?", Stratford Sherman, *Fortune*, December 13, 1993, p. 96.
2. "Managing Change: The Art of Balancing," Jeanie Daniel Duck, *Harvard Business Review*, November–December 1993, p. 110.

Chapter 16

1. "Strategic Intent," Gary and C. K. Prahalad, *Harvard Business Review*, May–June 1989, p. 63.
2. "Benchmarking: Lessons from the Best-in-Class," Rick Whiting, *Electronic Business*, October 7, 1991, p. 130.
3. "The Link between Benchmarking and Shareholder Value," Jeffrey A. Schmidt, *Journal of Business Strategy*, May–June 1992, p. 13.

Chapter 17

1. "Are You as Good as the Best in the World?", Stratford Sherman, *Fortune*, December 13, 1993, p. 96.
2. "How to Make Reengineering Really Work," Gene Hall, Jim Rosenthal, and Judy Wade, *Harvard Business Review*, November–December 1993, p. 126.
3. Ibid., p. 127.
4. Ibid., p. 129.
5. "Competing on Capabilities: The New Rules of Corporate Strategy," George Stalk, Philip Evans, and Lawrence E. Shulman, *Harvard Business Review*, March–April 1992, p. 58.
6. "Management's New Gurus," John A. Byrne, *Business Week*, August 31, 1992, p. 51.

Chapter 18

1. Paradise Visioning is loosely based on the term "Paradise Principle" used in the Price Waterhouse change methodology called Business Process Transformation.

Chapter 20

1. "How We Will Work in the Year 2000," Walter Kiechel III, *Fortune*, May 17, 1993, p. 40.
2. Ibid.
3. Ibid.
4. Tom Peters, *Liberation Management*, (New York: Alfred A. Knopf, 1992), p. 306.
5. "The Search for the Organization of Tomorrow," Thomas A. Stewart, *Fortune*, May 18, 1992, p. 93.
6. Ibid.

7. "Workplace of the Future: Effective Use of People Will Be Key to Company Success," *Ideas & Trends*, Issue 307, August 4, 1993, p. 126.
8. Ibid., p. 121.
9. "The Search for the Organization of Tomorrow," Thomas A. Stewart, *Fortune*, May 18, 1992, p. 94.
10. "How We Will Work in the Year 2000," Walter Kiechel III, *Fortune*, May 17, 1993, p. 44.
11. "The Search for the Organization of Tomorrow," Thomas A. Stewart, *Fortune*, May 18, 1992, p. 96.
12. Ibid.

Appendix A

1. Marion Mills Steeples, *The Corporate Guide to the Malcolm Baldrige National Quality Award*, ASQC Quality Press, 1993.
2. Ibid.
3. Ibid.
4. "TQM: More than a Dying Fad?", Rahul Jacob, *Fortune*, October 18, 1993, p. 66.

Appendix B

1. "Companies Find Savings with ISO 9000," Mark Morrow, *Quality Digest*, November, 1993, p. 22.

GLOSSARY

Adaptive Companies. A company that is able to adapt to rapidly changing environmental conditions with minimal effort and disruption to ongoing operations. Adaptive companies require use of an effective change management approach that is understood at every level of the corporation. They also require the ability to learn and then to institutionalize that learning.

Benchmarking. The process of comparing your organization and processes to world-class companies both within and outside your industry. Benchmarking's purpose is to identify best-of-class business practices for goal setting and process improvement, and to identify your company's relative operating effectiveness and efficiency.

Business Issues. Identifiable problems within the current process which are barriers to improvement, causes of inefficiencies, processing rules with no purpose, quality failures, lack of information, and any other condition that reduces performance.

Business Process Reengineering. The dramatic and discontinuous change to business processes; a complete reinvention of how work is done. BPT is defined by Michael Hammer as "the fundamental rethinking and radical redesign of business processes to achieve dramatic improvements in critical, contemporary measures of performance, such as cost, quality, service, and speed." Business Process Reengineering achieves equivalent results to the process value reinvention dimension of Total Process Management.

Case Worker. A worker who is trained with all the skills required to complete an entire process.

Cause-and-Effect Diagram. Also known as an Ishikawa or "fishbone" chart, cause-and-effect diagrams are powerful problem-solving tools used to examine factors that influence a given situation.

Cellular Workplace Design. Grouping together the people involved in a process to eliminate the problems inherent with physical separation, such as poor communication and batched work.

Change Actions. Actions required to bridge the gap between the current environment and the redesigned process.

Change Continuum. Total Process Management delivers change along the entire change continuum, from continuous and incremental change to dramatic and rapid change.

Change Drivers. The internal and external business conditions that "drive" the need to change.

Change Management. Any approach or methodology designed to support organizational change in order to achieve performance improvement can be considered to be change management. Total Process Management, Business Process Reengineering, and Total Quality Management are all change management methodologies.

Change Readiness Assessment. An analytical technique for evaluating an organization's commitment and capability to change.

Check Sheets. Simple forms for recording data that have been designed to allow interpreting the data from the form itself.

Command and Control Management. A style of management that involves controlling access to information at the management level and requiring most decisions be made or approved by management. It is part of the industrial management model that has been used widely since the turn of the 20th century.

Continuous Process Improvement. The constant and perpetual journey of improving quality and incorporating it into the very fabric of the business organization. This term is used synonymously with Total Quality Management and "quality culture." Continuous process improvement achieves equivalent results to the process value improvement dimension of Total Process Management.

Control Charts. Statistical tools that graphically display the normal (common causes) and abnormal variances (special causes) in processes.

Cycle Time. The total length of time required to produce a unit of output from beginning to end within a process. The term "speed" is often used in the place of cycle time, but has the same meaning.

Cycle Time Analysis. Cycle time is calculated by adding the elapsed times for all of the operations in a process. Analysis of this information can identify ways to shorten the overall cycle time for the process.

Decision Matrix. A tool for evaluating the pros and cons of several alternatives in order to select the best one.

Deployment Process Maps. The most common type of process map, which is used to show individuals, job titles, or departments across the top or down the side of the flowchart. The opposite axis represents time. Process symbols are shown in relation to the department where the work is performed.

Empowerment. Management practice where front-line employees are given both the authority and accountability to take necessary actions to achieve a particular goal. Management's responsibility shifts from assigning work and approving all decisions to advising employees on courses of action and removing barriers to the front-line employees' productivity.

Executive Sponsor. The person ultimately responsible for ensuring that Total Process Management is successful, both in its process improvement and process reinvention versions. This person is usually the CEO or highest-ranking business unit executive.

Force Field Analysis. An analytical technique formulated by Kurt Lewin for identifying underlying problem causes. "Forces" are listed in tabular form which either support (driving forces) or prevent (restraining forces) resolution.

Formal Hierarchy. An official organizational chart depicting who reports to whom.

Histogram. A type of chart that provides a graphic representation of variations in a set of data. Histograms are most effective for use in evaluating trends in large numbers of data.

Horizontal Corporations. Corporations that are run by cross-functional teams organized around business processes rather than functional departments. These business processes extend to both customers and suppliers. There are very few layers of management, and front-line workers have a high degree of responsibility and authority. The focus is on customers instead of bosses. All employees have free access to information, and training is emphasized.

Industrial Management Model. The American management philosophy of the post-World War II era when competition was negligible, resources were plentiful, and labor was cheap. This model involves management hierarchies, segmentation of jobs, and strict labor specialization.

Informal Hierarchy. An unofficial organizational chart that shows actual reporting structures, which may or may not be the same as the formal hierarchy. Informal hierarchies reveal the hidden layers of management.

Ishikawa Chart. Also known as a "fishbone" or "Cause-and-Effect" diagram, this problem-solving tool is used to examine all factors that may influence a given situation.

ISO 9000. ISO 9000 is the collective title for five international standards on quality management and compliance. See Appendix B for additional information.

Just-in-Time (JIT) Training. Companies provide training to employees only when they have an immediate and specific application of the material. In this way, it is easier to evaluate the results of the training, and the employees retain more of the material because it is reinforced immediately. Also called "performance-based training."

Kaizen. A Japanese term that means "gradual continuous improvement." This idea is the foundation for Total Quality Management and continuous improvement initiatives in the Western hemisphere.

Learning Organization. The concept of developing experts and creating expertise without the burden of bureaucracy.

Left-Brain Thinking. The left side of the brain is where analytical thinking and language are performed. Although this is essential for analysis, it is a hindrance to creativity.

Malcolm Baldrige National Quality Award. A national quality award to promote U.S. quality and productivity. See Appendix A for additional information.

Multi-voting. An analytical technique used to narrow down the potential causes of a problem to the top few. All potential causes are listed and voted upon. The ones with the most votes move to the next round. This process is repeated until the list is narrowed down to an acceptable number of causes.

One-Year Rule. Organizations generally are not capable of sustaining enthusiasm and interest in projects that last over one year. The "one-year rule" states that the process improvement teams should only tackle projects that can be completed within one year, or they should break the projects into pieces that can be completed in that time.

Operation. Any shape on a process map where an action occurs.

Paradise Visioning. A brainstorming activity where a process is completely redesigned to operate in the most effective and efficient manner possible.

Pareto Chart. A graphic representation of the 80-20 rule that helps to easily identify primary causes of problems with the best opportunities for improvement.

Pareto Principle. Joseph Juran's restatement of Vilfredo Pareto's *Maldistribution of Wealth Rule*. The Pareto Principle, also known as the 80-20 rule, states that most effects come from a relatively few causes.

Piggybacking. A technique in creative brainstorming where one or more ideas leads to other ideas.

Process. Processes are the systems of activities that collectively create value for customers. All processes have three elements: input, manipulation of the input, and output. Businesses are the sum total of all of their processes. These processes exist as an organic whole — it is very difficult to change one without affecting other parts of the business.

Process Cost Analysis. A method for determining the true cost of an entire process as it cuts across functional departments. Cost Accounting and Activity-Based Costing principles are used extensively in this analysis.

Process Flowchart. The basic unit of documentation required in order to understand and manage the effectiveness of business processes. Process flowcharts include inputs to the process and their sources, outputs from the process and their destinations, and all processing steps required to create the outputs.

Process Map. A form of flowchart that captures substantially more information than the standard process flowchart. Process maps also include certain characteristics (such as cycle time, task time, cost, units, quality index) that further define the process.

Process Member. Anyone who contributes to the activities in the process.

Process Owner. The process owner is responsible for ensuring that the total process is both effective and efficient, and that performance is continually improved.

Process Value Improvement (PVI). The dimension of Total Process Management that creates continuous incremental process improvement at the workgroup level. PVI delivers results equivalent to continuous process improvement.

PVI Workgroups. Process value improvement workgroups are temporary teams comprised of selected process members who come together to meet specific performance improvement objectives.

Process Value Reinvention (PVR). The dimension of Total Process Management that creates dramatic and rapid process improvement at the cross-departmental process level. PVR delivers results equivalent to Business Process Reengineering.

PVR Project Teams. Process value reinvention project teams are responsible for conducting the PVR projects and achieving the performance improvement objectives.

PVR Steering Committee. The process value reinvention steering committees have responsibility for monitoring progress of the process reinvention efforts, and for allocating resources and removing obstacles required for achieving the improvement goals. Also, the steering committee must evaluate and establish the priority of process reinvention projects.

Right-Brain Thinking. The right side of the brain is the source of creativity, imagination, and symbols. Right-brain thinking is essential for creativity, but it is frequently discouraged in the business world.

Run Chart. A simple statistical tool that plots data over time to identify trends.

Scatter Diagram. A statistical method for charting and analyzing the relationship between two variables.

Shewhart Cycle. An improvement approach used pervasively in the total quality arena for identifying, testing, and standardizing process improvements. Also known as the Plan-Do-Study-Act cycle.

Span of Control Analysis. A method for evaluating the organizational hierarchy. Span of control analysis is achieved by counting the number of people managing other employees and dividing that number into the total number of employees.

Stakeholder Analysis. An analytical approach for identifying individuals in the organization who have the most to gain or lose by the success or failure of a redesigned process.

Statistical Process Control. The application of statistical techniques for measuring and analyzing the variation in processes.

Structured Interviews. In this type of interview, the interviewers rigorously follow a prepared list of questions and give the interviewee little leeway to vary from the questions.

Team Design Sessions. Meetings in which members from each part of a process gather to jointly brainstorm process improvement opportunities.

TPM Facilitator/Coordinator. A person or department that reports to the executive sponsor and provides a number of services, including training and facilitation on the TPM methodology and monitoring and reporting on the progress of the change initiatives.

TPM Foundation. The Total Process Management foundation is comprised of parts 1 and 2 of the methodology. These two parts establish the corporate will and skills for change, respectively. The foundation supports the process improvement cycle.

TPM Process Improvement Cycle. The Total Process Management process improvement cycle is comprised of parts 3 through 7 of the methodology. These five parts comprise the recurring cycle of events required for effective process improvement (change) efforts.

TPM Steering Committee. The Total Process Management steering committee is responsible for initiating process value improvement throughout the organization, and for establishing the process value reinvention steering committee(s). The TPM steering committee is accountable to the executive sponsor for overall organizational acceptance of Total Process Management and for achieving tangible performance improvements through TPM.

Total Quality Management. The systematic integration of quality into every aspect of a company. This term is used synonymously with continuous process improvement and "quality culture."

Unstructured Interviews. In this kind of interview, interviewers provide loose guidelines and the interviewee shares information in the order that they choose.

Value-Added Ratio. The ratio of the time that adds customer value to the total process cycle time.

Virtual Organization. A structure that expands and contracts as necessary to conduct business as required. This organization hires experts or outsources non-essential activities when needed.

INDEX

Eating The Chocolate Elephant
Order Form

If you would like to order additional copies of *Eating the Chocolate Elephant*, you can let us know in three convenient ways.

1) Simply complete this form and drop it in the mail, or
2) Fax this form to the following number: 214-994-6475, or
3) Call toll-free: 1-800-998-1981 and talk to a "real live" service representative.

1-4 copies	_____	copies @ $24.95 per book
5-24 copies	_____	copies @ $22.95 per book
25-100 copies	_____	copies @ $19.95 per book
100-499 copies	_____	copies @ $16.95 per book
500 or more copies	_____	call for pricing

Name _____ Title _____

Organization _____ Phone _____

Street Address _____

City / State (Country) _____ Zip _____

Purchase Order Number (if applicable) _____

Applicable sales tax, shipping and handling charges will be added. Prices subject to change.

❑ Discovery   ❑ Visa   ❑ MasterCard   ❑ American Express

Account Number _____ Exp. Date _____

Signature _____

Mail to:
MetaSys Change Management Group
c/o Micrografx, Inc.
PO BOX 850358
Richardson, TX 75085-9954